RETURN TO KABUL

An Afghan American's Odyssey in Afghanistan

US Department of Defense Deployment
March 3, 2012–February 20, 2013

ABDULLAH SHARIF

To my dear friend Shaida.

A. Sharif

10-20-15

Disclaimers

Return to Kabul offers the public an insider's view of day-to-day activities in a combat zone and the challenges the US personnel face in Afghanistan. It's not intended to be "expert" in any way or to reflect the operations and projects of the US Departments of State and Defense in any way whatsoever.

Most importantly, it's a heartfelt memoir of the author's dual-country birth and life in Afghanistan and America, written with the sincere hope of furthering peace between both nations and around the world.

Copyright © 2015 Authored By Abdullah Sharif
All rights reserved.

ISBN: 0692432515
ISBN 13: 9780692432518

Additional Books by Abdullah Sharif

1. *Sardar: From Afghanistan's Golden Age to Carnage*
   Published July 17, 2014, by CreateSpace

1. *Kandahar Provincial Handbook: A Guide to the People and the Province*
   Published July 1, 2011, by IDS International

ENDORSEMENTS

Kandahar Office of the Governor deeply appreciates your outstanding collaboration and leadership efforts while you were the Political Director of KPRT (Kandahar Provincial Reconstruction Team).

Governor Tooryalai Wesa
Governor of Kandahar Province, Afghanistan

I had the pleasure of working with Abdullah Sharif when I was commander of ISAF (International Security Assistance Force) support for Afghanistan's Peace and Reintegration Process. His personal and professional experiences were invaluable to me and to senior leaders. Mr. Sharif helped us understand the nature of Afghan culture, sociopolitical interactions, and, most importantly, the relevant background and context to work in a country bedeviled by thirty-five years of conflict.

His sincere desire to improve a country mired in such turmoil was simply exemplary, and his personal courage, commitment, and professionalism were outstanding. He was also a confidant, adviser, and friend to me. Mr. Sharif's deep and thoughtful insights were profound (coming from personal experiences, no less, including numerous innovative approaches we might take into future campaigns), which benefited everyone, from policy and country experts to individuals who served at the humblest levels.

Mr. Sharif's book is invaluable for the international community, given his insights for developing practical, tactical strategies for Afghanistan's peace and rebuilding efforts.

Major General David A. Hook, CBE QCVS Royal Marines
Deputy Commander RC(S), Kandahar, October 2008–November 2009
Commander ISAF FRIC, Kabul, September 2011–October 2012

Although I didn't work directly with Mr. Sharif while in Kandahar, I witnessed firsthand his dedication and thirst for change in Afghanistan through my late father, Mayor Ghulam Haider Hamidi of Kandahar City, who sacrificed his life in 2011 while serving there. Mr. Sharif pays a poignant tribute to my father in this book. Readers will benefit from the author's thoughts on accounts and analyses, which put his book above political and military machinations. It's an eye-opening collection of missives by an Afghan American patriot, concerned world citizen, and peace advocate.

Rangina Hamidi
Founder and Creative Director, Kandahar Treasure

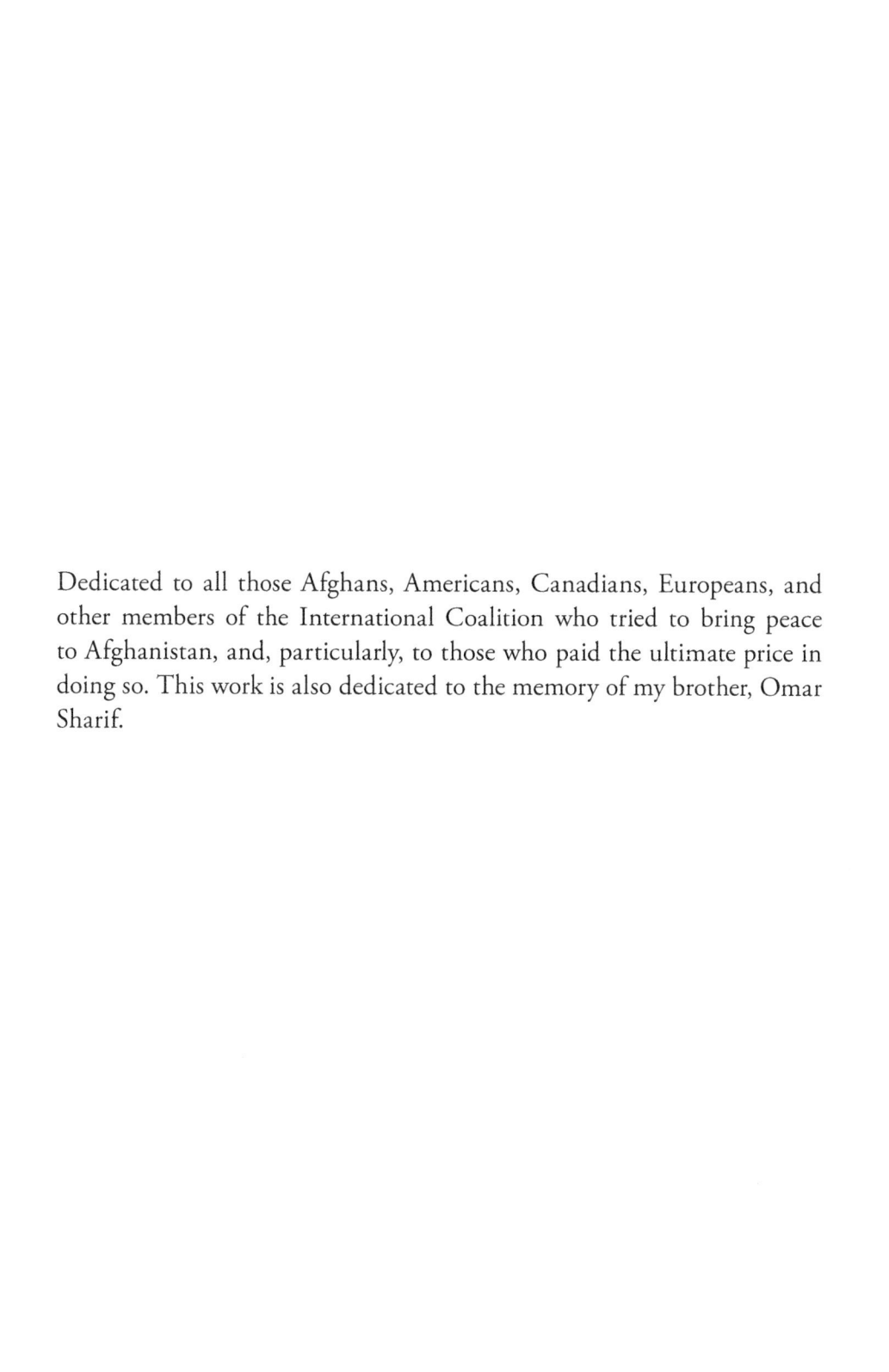

Dedicated to all those Afghans, Americans, Canadians, Europeans, and other members of the International Coalition who tried to bring peace to Afghanistan, and, particularly, to those who paid the ultimate price in doing so. This work is also dedicated to the memory of my brother, Omar Sharif.

ACKNOWLEDGMENTS

The core of this work consists of many missives that I penned during my two tours of duty in Afghanistan. The aim was to give my family and friends an idea about my daily life and challenges there. My wife and my first editor, Catherine, deserves huge credit as she patiently edited my missives and distributed them via e-mail to the recipients. She also designed and launched my website. She gathered, scanned, and organized many pictures that I have used in the book and on the website. Many of these pictures tell the story of Afghanistan's Golden Age.

I had no idea that I would eventually expand on the recounting of my experiences in Afghanistan to produce the book. The first encouragement came from many family members and friends who believed that I had a worthwhile story to tell. My sincere thanks go to all those who believed in me. I would like to particularly thank my father-in-law, Edward Connelly, without whose extraordinary support I would not have been able to undertake and complete this project.

I am so fortunate to have the support and unconditional love of my mother, Hamida, and my sisters, Hosai, Homa, Shaima, Zarmina, Tooba, and Zarlasht. Special thanks to my brother, Belal, who has been very respectful and supportive all along. I would also like to mention my appreciation for all of my many nephews and nieces. I am especially grateful to my nephew Tareck Safi, who provided many invaluable suggestions for the work.

TABLE OF CONTENTS

Part 2 ~ US Department of Defense Deployment, 3.1.2012–2.20.2013

Prologue
    Growing Up in Afghanistan, When the Going Was Good ····· xxi

Chapter 1   7.27.2011
    Tribute to Ghulam Haidar Hamidi, Mayor of Kandahar City ··· 1

Chapter 2   3. 12. 2012
    My Second Deployment as a GS-15 Civilian ················ 5

Chapter 3   3.20.2012
    The Taliban Promote a Culture of Intimidation
        and Corruption ···························· 11

Chapter 4   4.3.2012
    Stalled by Military Bureaucracy ························ 17

Chapter 5   4.19.2012
    Revisiting Camp Nathan Smith and Kandahar Province ······ 23

Chapter 6   5.13.2012
    Three Months of DOD Deployment—with Nothing
        to Show for It ···························· 29

Chapter 7   6.2.2012
    Why is Promoting Peace Such a Pipe Dream? ············· 35

Chapter 8   7.22.2012
   Gearing Up for HPC Activities · 41

Chapter 9   8.14.2012
   Promoting Diplomacy in Advancing HPC's
          Goal for Reconciliation · 49

Chapter 10   8.21.2012
   Afghans Celebrate Holidays with Gusto! · · · · · · · · · · · · · · · · · · 55

Chapter 11   9.4.2012
   Modifying Perceptions for Afghanistan's Peaceful
          Socioeconomic Transition · 61

Chapter 12   9.18.2012
   Children Are Extinguished, Like Moths Drawn to a
          Deadly Flame· 67

Chapter 13   10.1.2012
   High Peace Council Takes the High Road to Peace · · · · · · · · · · · 73

Chapter 14   11.21.2012
   Effective Leaders Must Be Determined Movers and Shakers· · · · 81

Chapter 15   12.19.2012
   Preparing to Draw Down Peacefully from Afghanistan · · · · · · · 87

Chapter 16   2.1.2013
   Final Impressions· 95

Chapter 17   3.15.2013
   My Second Tour in Afghanistan Ends · · · · · · · · · · · · · · · · · · · 101

Chapter 18   5.10.2014
   My Stint at CENTCOM · 105

Chapter 19   3.4.2015
   Afghanistan in Transition · 109

Photo Gallery · 120

Author Bio · 129

Appendices
   Afghan Cultural Terms · 131
   Acronyms · 133
   Mohammadzai Family Tree · 137

FOREWORD

A peace diplomat and citizen of the world rooted in Eastern (Afghanistan) and Western (American) sensibilities, Abdullah Sharif successfully captures the essence of how cultural changes acutely transform individuals and societies—in the twinkling of a few years.

Having lived the good life growing up during Afghanistan's Golden Age from the 1950s to mid-1970s, Abdullah's reminiscences are touchstones for historians, military strategists, and general readers.

The contributions of memoirists are many. They clarify situations. They provide background and relevant contexts for readers to glean revealing insights through informed analyses. Abdullah's first memoir, *Sardar*, contributes to our understanding of how complicated, multifaceted Afghan tribal customs collude and yet, surprisingly, can be helpful when conditions dictate the need for unified actions impacting the whole country.

This timely memoir describes how the author, after coming to America and achieving the American Dream, became committed to giving back to both his birth and adopted countries by making his vision for a very personal "Afghanistan Project" a reality. This memoir answers many interesting questions: What drives Abdullah to become a peace diplomat? What obstacles frustrate his attempts? How can military, political, and socioeconomic operations return rule of law to a country ripped apart by incessant wars—not only presently, but also from centuries past? How can Afghans start taking steps toward building a peaceful, productive republic?

This author's compassion and astute analyses offer simple, commonsense insights to inspire innovative and practical alliances and cooperation. All these insights could work toward fulfilling his aching hope of reconciliation among Afghanistan's myriad tribal clans—by sowing the seeds of peace and prosperity. But might this be only a pipe dream?

Readers of this memoir are privy to poignant observations, such as Abdullah's appreciation of his privilege in escaping the horrors of war—compared to three picnicking Tajik boy soldiers who were literally born manacled into war's captivity.

Abdullah's dual destinies have awakened in him the responsibilities of selflessly serving as best he can in two very disparate societies. His observations are priceless for rebuilding Afghanistan and for exhorting the international community toward effective peace-building and peace-keeping cooperation and initiatives.

Readers will gain an appreciation for their roles as responsible world citizens and stewards in building strong socioeconomic and political foundations for posterity's sake.

Tooryalai Wesa, PhD
Governor of Kandahar Province, Afghanistan

INTRODUCTION

My first book, *Sardar: From Afghanistan's Golden Age to Carnage,* recounts my deployment in Afghanistan from October 2009 to January 2011. As a US State Department civilian, I was determined to contribute as much as I could for a cause I believed was the most important foreign policy and national security challenge our country faced. This challenge was even more daunting for Afghanistan, the country of my birth, to surmount in making progress toward peaceful nation-building.

As an Afghan American, having grown up in Afghanistan and become an American citizen as an adult, I have one foot in the West and one foot in the East. Additionally, I have a baseline with which to compare what the country looks like today as opposed to when it was once a viable nation-state. I believe that there are many lessons to be learned from the proper Afghan context from the past that could be used by the international community, including the International Security and Assistance Force (ISAF), the United Nations, the US Agency for International Development (USAID), and nongovernmental organizations (NGOs), for a better outcome in the country. Many experts in America and those who served in Afghanistan mainly attribute the current Afghan problems to ethnic and tribal diversity and the competition between tribes. However, the ethnic and tribal nature of Afghan society is nothing new. Despite this, Afghanistan was a functional nation-state during the Golden Age, roughly between the 1930s and 1970s, despite the existence of the same ethnic and tribal challenges. There are only a handful of people like me who can explain why Afghanistan functioned so well during that period; I was a product of that golden era. Obviously the lessons of history are always constrained by differences in time and space, but they are still very relevant in trying to place the problems in the right frame of reference in order to be able to devise the right solution. So I entered service with the US State Department feeling that I was uniquely positioned as a resource to make a difference in the endeavor to put the questions in the right context and bridge the gap between the Afghans and the Western organizations trying to bring peace to the country and rebuild Afghanistan.

Originally my tour with the State Department was for one year. However, as a result of the insistence of my State Department colleagues in Kandahar, the late Mayor Hamidi, the governor, and others, I extended my tour for several months more. My intention was to return home and continue my contribution to the Afghan mission at the State Department, where most policies relative to Afghanistan are formulated and decisions are made. In fact, I thought that my input would be even more valuable as a force multiplier, rather than only specific to our work in Kandahar where I served. Upon my arrival back in the United States in January 2011 and in subsequent months, I had interviews at the office of the Special Representative for Afghanistan and Pakistan. But to my surprise and disappointment, I received an e-mail from the Afghanistan Desk at the US State Department informing me that they were not interested in me and could not offer me a position. This is where office politics come into play. The typical foreign service officer at the Afghanistan Desk might be threatened by an outsider who may know more about Afghanistan than he or she knows. I had been in this situation before when I first arrived in Kandahar, but colleagues soon realized that I was not in competition with them as my career was already behind me and my only aim was to help in any way I could.

After the negative response from the State Department, I continued my work on Afghanistan, first through IDS International, a private company, and then as a consultant. However, I wanted to return to Afghanistan as I thought that I would be more effective as a go-between for the US and Afghan sides, similar to what I did during my first tour. I therefore decided to join the US Department of Defense through the Civilian Expeditionary Force. More specifically, I joined the Defense Department's Afghanistan-Pakistan (AfPak) program.

This second book, *Return to Kabul: An Afghan American's Odyssey in Afghanistan*, shares missives I penned to family and friends during my second tour of duty in Kabul with the US Department of Defense from

March 3, 2012, to February 20, 2013. I was a GS-15 civilian employee, equivalent in rank to an O-6 or colonel. I soon found out that civilians don't carry the same weight as military personnel regardless of rank. It took a while for me to find my footing, as I describe in later chapters, but eventually I worked alongside my military colleagues at the ISAF Headquarters (HQ ISAF) in support of peace and reconciliation.

This book is the continuation of my first book, *Sardar: From Afghanistan's Golden Age to Carnage*. Sardar is the aristocratic name of my Mohammadzai clan, which ruled Afghanistan for most of its modern history since 1747. This clan has a mixed record, some good and some bad. But, the Golden Age of Afghanistan was a result of their efforts along with the efforts of many other Afghans of various tribal and ethnic affiliations, which many elderly Afghans still remember. Although neither I nor my father used the title, when Afghans in Kandahar and later in Kabul found out about my family affiliation, some would call me Sardar Sahib over my objections. But, they explained to me that my family has left behind a legacy which they want to acknowledge. My State Department colleagues would also at times jokingly call me Sardar. See the appendix for more information on my family.

I'm privileged to continue to share my experiences as an Afghan American going back to a chaotic Afghanistan. My hope is to offer a view from a different perspective for readers to better understand the current affairs in Afghanistan and the challenges we face in nation-building. I can be reached at: contact@AbdullahSharif.com.

Although this book is about my second deployment, the first chapter begins with a tribute to the late Mayor Hamidi of Kandahar City with whom I worked very closely during my first deployment with the Department of State. It would have been more appropriate to include the tribute in *Sardar: From Afghanistan's Golden Age to Carnage*, but an editorial mistake prevented it.

PROLOGUE

Growing Up in Afghanistan, When the Going Was Good

On a chilly late April morning in 1955 when spring buds were ushering in the new season, my nineteen-year-old mother Hamida gave birth to a lively, feisty second baby. My father, Mohammad Sharif, was then a forty-three-year-old "Ghund Misher" or deputy commander of Afghanistan's Royal Guard stationed at Arg, the Royal Palace in Kabul. I was their first son, born two years after my older sister, Zarmina.

At the age of five, I started first grade in Kabul's Masood Sad Elementary School. By then, my father was a full colonel and brigade commander in Gomal, a desolate, godforsaken place in east Afghanistan on the Pakistani border.

The war of words was heating up between Afghanistan and Pakistan over Pashtunistan and the disputed Durand Line. It was imperative to send a signal to Pakistan. This Line was an imaginary demarcation imposed in 1893 by then British Foreign Secretary in India, Sir Mortimer Durand, and the Amir of Afghanistan. When Pakistan achieved independence from India in 1947, this Line became the de facto border between Afghanistan and Pakistan—and remains a source of friction between both countries up to today.

Sardar Daoud Khan, Afghanistan's Prime Minister and Defense Minister at the time, was also King Zahir Shah's first cousin. He personally asked my father to take up peaceful arms in Gomal. A patriot and military hero, my father agreed (and sacrificed family life for service to country). Thus, we didn't see much of him while growing up.

Trips back and forth to his post took at least a day by four-wheel-drive vehicles. Father came to see us occasionally, sometimes arriving in the middle of the night in his Russian-made military vehicle with his driver. We'd wake up rejoicing that he was home.

On every return trip, my father loaded up his vehicle with saplings, flowering bushes, and various kinds of shrubbery. Father had decided that instead of waiting at the border in temporary accommodations for war to break out with Pakistan, he'd build permanent quarters for his officers and conscripts.

By the time his tour ended, my father had inadvertently built a town around the military base. Officers deployed there with their families, and a school was built. The saplings and flower bushes became welcome havens and gardens for their families. In fact, some locals tried to change the town's name to Sharif Kot ("Sharif's Place"). A local poet was even moved to compose a poem about Sharif Kot and its founder, Mohammad Sharif.

While my father was away, my mother continued her full-time midwife's job at Zayeshgah Maternity Hospital. We didn't like it when she covered night shifts and threw crying fits, which probably made her job even more difficult. A wet nurse cared for us.

In addition to Zarmina, my siblings included sisters and a brother from my father's first marriage. Their mother, Mahboob Jan, had died of tuberculosis. In Afghan society, "half siblings" are part of the integral family and everyone gets along amicably (except for occasional spats like any family). My older sisters, Hosai and Homa, went to a girls' high school, Zarghoona, while Shaima attended Malalai for girls. My older brother, Omar, went to Habibia, Kabul's oldest boys' high school, where I also later went. After me came my brother Belal; some years later, my sisters Tooba and Zarlasht. I idolized Omar, who taught me hunting, driving, and manly pursuits; he also taught my mother how to drive.

A fringe benefit Afghan military officers enjoyed at that time was to have two male conscripts serve in their households. At our home, one was in charge of cooking, while the other cleaned and did household chores under my mother's supervision. It was on-the-job training for these young men. They didn't have the requisite skills when they started, but became proficient cooks and butlers after finishing household tours of duty. The cycle started anew every two years. Life in households for conscripts was much better than life in the barracks.

My father retired from the military when I was in sixth grade. He had type 2 diabetes and couldn't continue. (He possibly left because of political reasons, too.) That was an important year for me. I learned to drive, starting with our Volkswagen Beetle and later with a white Volkswagen Squareback. On weekends, Omar, my mom, and I went to Bagrami, southeast of Kabul, where a flat golf course with hardly anyone around beckoned—and provided us the perfect driving school grounds.

At twelve, I wasn't tall enough to see over the steering wheel. I'd put a pillow on the seat, which worked well given my long legs and shorter torso. One day, mother got a call from a friend, the principal of Rabia Balkhi girls' high school near our house. She'd seen our car in motion without a driver. But when it came up closer, she saw me driving, peering up while being barely visible. She asked my mother never to let me drive a car again. But my mother reassured her I was a good driver and there was nothing to fear.

In seventh grade (at an all-boys school), our English teacher was an attractive young, blond Peace Corps volunteer. Miss Fisher cycled to school dressed in pretty flowery dresses. We eagerly looked forward to her class and savored her tantalizing presence—gratified that she filtered away the noxious air other teachers left behind.

I think Miss Fisher was my earliest inspiration to choose the United States as my adopted country over European ones. At the time, you don't think about how such incidents impact your sensibilities. Too, people don't realize how important it is to always make a positive impact in someone's life. It may not have been immediately apparent but in looking back, it affected me indelibly. Miss Fisher taught us more than grammar, sentence structure, and English words. She talked about her way of life back home—even explaining the education system enough to where we knew about PTA meetings. Miss Fisher gracefully epitomized President John F. Kennedy's vision of creating the Peace Corps to spread America's high ideals around the world.

In the late 1960s to early 1970s, King Zahir Shah began liberalizing Afghan society. Mass proliferation of free expression in the newspapers and political parties ensued.

Left-leaning parties like Parcham ("banner") and Khalq ("people") were instigated by the Soviet Union while Shola Jawid ("immortal torch") was Maoist-inspired. These parties recruited high schoolers and organized demonstrations disrupting classes for weeks.

These parties weren't only critical of government and monarchy, but also busily denounced each other. Those of us who didn't participate took advantage of their disruptions to ditch school and drive around town until it was time to return home at about 1:00 p.m.

Another Peace Corps volunteer who affected me deeply was Thomas Gouttierre, my English teacher and basketball coach during eighth and ninth grades. Tom later returned to Afghanistan as a Fulbright Scholar and established the Center for Afghanistan Studies at the University of Nebraska in Omaha in 1972.

In summer 1973, we hosted Jim Pressler, an AFS (American Foreign Student) exchange student from Cleveland, Ohio. Jim and I hit it right off! One fateful night that memorable summer, I was sound asleep when Jim woke me up at about 3:00 a.m. Gunfire and heavy equipment traffic trundled along on the street below us. I told him there was nothing to worry about, that perhaps they were preparing for the upcoming Independence Day celebrations and military parade. Back then, we weren't used to the sounds of gunfire in Afghanistan, so I didn't pay much attention to what was going on. We fell right back to sleep.

But in the morning, the radio played only music, nothing else. Then, out of the blue, we heard an announcement that Sardar Mohammad Dauod Khan would be addressing the nation momentarily. We knew then something big had happened.

Afghanistan's new leader announced in a deep lumbering voice he and his comrades had over thrown the monarchy—that Afghanistan had become a republic. He reassured the nation everything was under control. It was July 17, 1973. Although gunfire had broken out, this was a bloodless coup and no one was killed. But many people were very disturbed and unsettled, including my father and uncles.

Out daily routine didn't change much thereafter. Except for a few months when we were followed by an unmarked car, especially when we went to see our uncle Arif Khan.

The summer of 1973 went by very quickly and the time arrived for Jim and the other AFS students to leave for home. The night before Jim's departure, we sat on our beds and talked for a long, long time, shedding tears. The next day, Jim dressed in Afghan tunic and baggy pants; we took him to the airport. Bidding him adieu was very emotional for our family, even though he'd only stayed with us three months.

That year, 1973, was also my senior year. I finished school in December, getting by with minimum effort. The biggest thing after graduation was taking the university entrance exam, "concours," French for competition. My friends studied hard for weeks preceding it, but I decided against wasting time. I reasoned concours was meant to determine a person's general knowledge spanning the past twelve years of education. If I'd not learned anything up to then, how'd I be able to cram all that knowledge in just a few weeks preparing for it?

Instead, I went to Jalalabad where our winter home was, returning to Kabul on the evening before the exam. My cousin Hamid and my other buddies were still hard at work, cramming away. The next day, we went to Kabul University for the exam. It was hard. Competition was intense; thousands of graduating seniors across the whole country competed for a couple of thousand spots.

Just to hedge my bets, in the meantime, my parents sent me to France where I enrolled at the University of Bordeaux. I stayed in a rental there. Zarmina and Noor, her physician husband, also lived in Bordeaux. One spring day in 1974, my father called to say I'd passed concours and was accepted by the engineering school. I should return, he said.

Kabul University's Engineering School had probably the toughest curriculum. Every subject was taught in English either by American professors or Afghans with PhDs from the best American universities. Textbooks were from the United States, too. I spent more time there studying to barely tread above water. I sputtered along, passing some exams while failing others. One semester, I couldn't attend classes because I didn't have the required grade point average and was penalized.

But we had a great time partying at Kabul University! Girls came to school in miniskirts and partied with us; we played basketball and card games and sometimes went out drinking. I had my own car, a great white Citroen Deux Chevaux (Duck) that even took us to Bamiyan in central Afghanistan where huge Buddha statues were carved into mountainsides fifteen hundred years ago (but were destroyed by the Taliban in July 1999).

My father's health got progressively worse in 1976. He left for India with my mother for medical treatment in June. When he returned, he was still ill. My mother continued nursing him, but his eyesight worsened. He was hospitalized, but he wanted to go to Paghman, where our summer home was.

One weekend while some of us were attending a wedding in Kabul, my father had problems breathing. We rushed him to Iben Sina (Avicenna) Hospital in Kabul. Father was put on a stretcher headed to the ER. I placed an oxygen mask over his face, and his breathing eased a bit. I asked him how he felt; he said "better." The doctors poured in and hooked him up to various machines.

But suddenly, my father stopped breathing; the doctors started resuscitating tactics with CPR and a defibrillator. I couldn't take it and left, knowing full well that was the end. Out in the hospital courtyard, relatives started arriving. My mother's youngest brother, Uncle Sultan, asked me how my father was. I responded: "Dead." I'm not sure my uncle believed me as he rushed inside to find out for himself.

My father's body was washed and prepared for burial according to Islamic tradition that same night. He was wrapped in white cotton cloth, placed in a simple coffin, and brought home to spend his last night with us. He was sixty-four. There was pandemonium in our house that night of August 16, 1976. Unfortunately, it was also my youngest sister Zarlasht's seventh birthday.

The next morning, my father was buried with full military honors. It was the biggest funeral I'd ever attended. Father's friend General Haidar Rasooli, Minister of Defense, drove us in his limousine in the cortege. There were two sessions the following two days at Haji Yaqub Mosque for people to pay their last respects. Similar events for women were held at a different venue.

My father, and also my mother to a lesser degree, was strict and held very conservative views, but they never imposed those views on us. They never told us we had to pray five times a day, fast, or dress as Muslims. My sisters dressed as they pleased in the latest fashions without even donning simple headscarves, let alone wear the burqa. My sisters, cousins, and mother were not alone; other younger Kabuli women were also fashionably dressed and kept up with the times.

There were no western NGOs or governments educating and lecturing Afghans on women's rights. It was a natural societal progression toward modernism within the Afghan context at the time. Was it comparable to the west? Absolutely not. Was it practiced throughout the country? Nope, just in larger cities like Kabul. But it was the beginning of a new era—which most regrettably died on the vine.

My father's death totally devastated us. I became extremely depressed and cried inconsolably every day. I dropped out of school. I thought the best option was to leave the country to continue my studies abroad. Leaving my family, younger sisters, and brother may have been construed as cowardice. My older brother Omar was married and busy with his family. At the end of the day, I unequivocally decided to leave.

I left Kabul on November 3, 1976, on a crisp, bright day. As was customary, immediate family members drove to the airport to see me off. The Ariana Afghan Airlines flight was on time. That evening, I landed in Paris to build a new life—far away from Afghanistan, the land of my birth, which had gifted me a very happy childhood. Unbeknownst to me then, the next time I'd set foot there would be thirty-one years later—as a citizen of the United States of America. And later as a US State Department diplomat entrusted with rebuilding a war-torn Afghanistan and building peace bridges between Afghans and Americans.

I'm very grateful to have had the opportunity to strive to be like my father, to engage in similar yet dissimilar paths toward peaceful goals. Mohammad Sharif, brigade commander of Afghanistan's Royal Guard, sacrificed family life to maintain Afghanistan's sovereignty in the face of Pakistani threats.

Abdullah Sharif, aviation engineer turned peace diplomat, has come full circle in writing this memoir to better understand why he's committed to building peace bridges across continents and between east and west. I'm also blessed with my marriage to Catherine Connelly and to be a part of her family, all of whom have inspired me.

I know my father would've been very happy and proud, as is my mother.

My Heart Bleeds for Afghanistan's Recovery
My Return to Kabul in April 2007 ~ After 30 Years

These days, Kabul and Afghanistan evoke a picture of chaos, war, and terrorism—including both human and material devastation. What I witnessed upon my return thirty years later, I couldn't have imagined in my wildest nightmares!

I'd been contemplating returning to Kabul since the fall of the Taliban in 2001. I was ambivalent because I didn't want to spoil my happy memories of the Golden Age, which lasted from 1930 to the mid-1970s.

Finally, however, the desire to see what had transpired got the better of me, so I finally returned for a brief visit in April 2007.

To understand Afghanistan in the twenty-first century, it's essential to know how this now-infamous city looked three decades ago before the events that unfolded so cruelly and reshaped my birth country.

The End of Afghanistan's Golden Age

In 1973, Afghanistan became a republic because of a bloodless coup d'état. It brought to an end the forty-year constitutional monarchy of King Zahir Shah, one of the longest reigning monarchs in Afghan history. Sardar Mohammad Daoud, the coup leader, was the king's first cousin who'd once been prime minister and a respected leader.

Some foresaw the coup as the lead up to the inevitable end of Afghanistan's Golden Age. There were at least two reasons the coup ended in disaster. First, Afghanistan was, and still is, a traditional society; for, although it had seen modernization culturally and socio-economically, its people weren't ready to welcome a self-governing republic just yet.

Second, President Daoud's government was comprised of mostly incompetent and untrained junior army officers, without any history to guide them and totally inexperienced in governing effectively. Worse, some were recruited by the Soviet KGB and revolted against Daoud in a bloody coup five years later.

Kabul in the mid-1970s had a population of about 650,000. It was a charming city of resplendent palaces, gardens, trees, parks, and Hollywood-style movie theaters. A network of tree-lined, grand paved roads connected various sections of the city. Some locals wore traditional garb. Many Kabulis dressed in suits, dresses, miniskirts, and the latest trendy 1970s fashions including platform shoes and bell-bottomed pants. Travel was safe—even to the remotest areas at any time of day or night.

But the Golden Age came to an abrupt end in April 1978 when President Daoud was brutally killed, along with most of his family members. This coup was organized by the Russian KGB—but carried out by members of the Afghan army who'd joined the Khalq and Parcham communist parties. These two parties were bitter rivals, but nevertheless they joined forces to drive out Daoud.

Suddenly, a reign of terror began all at once: there were mass arrests, torture (Abu Ghraib's excesses would be a picnic!), summary executions, confiscation of property, and trampling on of people's religious rights and cultural beliefs.

Not surprisingly, an Afghan national uprising against the communists began.

In the meantime, past rivalries of the Khalq and Parcham parties resurfaced. Infighting ensued, with the Khalqis getting the upper hand. The Khalqis marginalized the Parcham leaders (former government leaders in Kabul) by dispatching them to Eastern European Block countries as Afghanistan's ambassadors.

Moscow grew increasingly dissatisfied with the Khalqis and, particularly, with Hafizullah Amin, who'd killed Khalqi Afghan President Noor Mohammad Taraki in a palace coup—then declared himself the new Afghan president. Moscow blamed Amin for the deteriorating situation and the increasingly militant national uprisings (that Afghans called "jihad" against the communist unbelievers). Moscow worried that the Afghan national uprising would soon remove the pro-Soviet communist government from power. Thus the Kremlin saw no choice but to prop up the regime in Afghanistan according to the "The Brezhnev Doctrine"—at any cost Moscow saw fit—similar to what had happened in Hungary in 1956 and Czechoslovakia in 1968. This Doctrine was a mandate to support friendly puppet regimes the Kremlin had installed.

Moscow had another card to play, which was to bring the Parcham faction to power. The plan was to blame the Khalqis for everything that had gone wrong (including the tortures and other excesses) in hopes of easing anxiety and stopping the national uprising.

On Christmas Eve 1979, the Red Army crossed the ancient Oxus River (Amu Daria) to prop up the Soviet's Afghan puppets with an overt intervention. Babrak Karmal, the Parcham leader who'd been appointed ambassador to Czechoslovakia, expediently returned home with the first Soviet Special Forces airlifted to Kabul. The Soviet

Special Forces went directly to Tajbeg Palace where President Amin lay semiconscious; they delivered the final coup de grâce, execution-style. With Karmal and the Soviets in cahoots, a new phase began in accelerating Afghanistan's irrevocable downward spiral.

Ten years later, one million Afghans were dead, five million were displaced to neighboring countries (primarily Pakistan and Iran), and previously lush, fertile lands were rendered useless by millions of land mines; the defeated Red Army left Afghanistan for good on February 16, 1989. What was left behind was not good. Russia's weakened economy was a major factor in America winning the Cold War. The United States, Saudi Arabia, and others poured billions of dollars of military aid into Afghanistan. Pakistan was the conduit for these operations. Unwittingly, such vested interests would prove very detrimental to the world later on, with the creation of the Taliban.

Afghanistan's journey toward the abyss continued after the Red Army's retreat: First, infighting between various groups, such as among the "mujahedeen," who were nominal allies during the Soviet occupation. Afghans who fought the Soviets were mujahedeen. (A "mujaheed" commits to "jihad" by fighting others to defend his religion, country, and way of life.) A handful of politically active military mujahedeen groups in Pakistan, supported by the United States, threw out the Soviets. These groups ranged from moderate Mahaz-e-Mili monarchists to hard-line Hizb-e-Islami, headed by Gulbudin Hekmatyar, a notorious terrorist.

These groups were "allies" only in name—for the sole purpose of driving out the enemy. In truth, they were very diverse in their political and religious ideas and in their agendas for staying in power, as well. Once the common goal of vanquishing the Soviets was achieved, there were no other common interests left to promote cohesive nation-building among the mujahedeen. This, unfortunately, led to infighting for the control of Afghanistan.

Although the Soviet Union had left, Afghanistan's last communist president, Doctor Najibullah, clung to power until March 1992.

Various mujahedeen groups tried to establish a coalition government to rebuild Afghanistan, but were unable to because of their deep divisions. Infighting caused lots of hardship for locals in large cities, especially Kabul. Most of Kabul was destroyed during this time, too. People grew sick and tired of such lawlessness!

Pakistan had supported the various mujahedeen parties, especially hard-liners such as Hizb-e-Islami. The Pakistani government felt that Pakistan's vested interests in a post-Soviet Afghanistan were in jeopardy since they couldn't count on the mujahedeen and had lost control over them.

However, Pakistan had a Plan B in the works for many years: the Taliban. The Taliban (Islamic "seekers"), supported and encouraged by Pakistan, took advantage of Afghans' general dissatisfaction. Conditions were therefore ripe in 1994 for the Taliban to start their own conquest of Afghanistan.

The Taliban were able to disarm mujahedeen groups that were pillaging and raping the population. People were also relieved that stray rockets were no longer lobbed by various factions against each other. BUT—people didn't know that the Taliban didn't have viable means of governing the country, creating jobs, nor introducing a rule of law and peaceful means for Afghanistan's recovery. Instead, the situation worsened.

The Taliban also played a very extreme version of Islam with a skewed interpretation of what the religion is about. One reason they were able to bring about a semblance of security was by imposing a brutal rule of law. They started public executions of people who were accused of adultery and other crimes, without having to go through legal due process.

Therefore, in 1995, another reign of terror came about for Afghans when Taliban insurgents, created by and in Pakistan from pools of Afghan refugees in Saudi-funded religious schools ("madrassas"), took over the country. These Taliban were accompanied by Al-Qaeda, which consisted of various radicals from different national backgrounds who'd flocked to Pakistan to fight against the Soviets in Afghanistan. These groups called themselves "Muslims." Their dark legacies in Afghanistan and elsewhere clearly showed they were anything but spiritual seekers.

The Taliban entered Kabul on September 27, 1996. Many in Kabul, then and today, convulse at hearing this name. Sadly, they're making a strong comeback today.

Sick and anxious with anticipation, I boarded the Kam Air flight with my mother, Hamida Sharif. Two and a half hours later, the aircraft made the usual banking downward movement toward Kabul International Airport. Kabul is about the same altitude as Denver and is also surrounded by mountain ranges. (As an aside, Russian planes had had to take off and descend in a corkscrew maneuver to avoid being hit by anti-air rockets of mujahedeen resistance fighters lurking on the ridges.)

After a short walk across the tarmac, we entered the terminal building. Instantly, the Afghanistan of its Golden Age I'd cherished in my heart for so many years was shattered! It was April 10, 2007, at around 10:30 a.m. Chaos was the order of the day. From the disorderly passport control desk to the melee around the one rickety conveyor belt and piles of luggage, which left little room to move about, claiming our bags that day was a hopeless cause. Over the next two days, I returned twice to claim all our luggage.

At the airport, we were greeted by a man and his son who cared for my mother's property in Kabul. We hired an old yellow and white right-hand drive car, which had seen better days in Pakistan. Kabulis drive on the right side of the road. But many right-hand drive cars were brought in from Pakistan, where traffic flows on the left side of the road. The harrowing ride to downtown Kabul, just four miles from the airport, took over half an hour. It gave me a preview of what the city had become—and experiences yet to come.

In the first decade of the twenty-first century, Kabul's population had soared close to five million. The vast majority of the population was returning refugees and impoverished country folk in search of safety and jobs. Most roads leading into and out of the city and along the boulevards were devoid of trees. The Soviets and warring Afghan factions cut down the trees to eliminate hiding places for their enemies. The remaining trees became fuel for unfortunate Kabulis who suffered in the cold (and also went hungry) during Taliban rule from 1996 until the Taliban's fall in 2001.

Roads and neighborhood streets, once paved and drivable, had disintegrated into dirt paths or were in abominable states of disrepair. Roads were constantly jammed with cars spewing forth noxious fumes and kicking up fine dust particles, making it difficult to breathe. Traffic conditions were chaotic at best, with pedestrians, pushcarts, bicycles, motorcycles, and animals loaded with cargo moving helter-skelter in all directions. Cacophonous sounds of vehicles honking, along with the traffic police blaring over loud speakers, were crude and deafening. Strangely, I didn't witness any accidents. Order in chaos?

Poor Kabul had grown willy-nilly, with an unplanned sprawl in all directions, dotted with mud huts housing people and businesses. There was no running water or sewage systems, except in a limited number of neighborhoods.

The prevailing disorder provided a wild juxtaposition of contrasts that assaulted my eyes, ears, and senses. Satellite dishes and cell phones were in abundance. Sidewalks were teeming with all manner of mercantile offerings, from women's undergarments to fruits, vegetables, and cell phone cards. Money changers, who carried stacks of cash to exchange for foreign currencies, shared space with beggars crying out for handouts. The sidewalks were also home to manned desktop computers, which were used to upload images and music into customers' cell phones.

New office buildings and hotels catered to the growing foreign population and returning expatriates who could afford them. In some neighborhoods, Western restaurants housed in walled former villas were mostly frequented by a Western clientele—with armed guards at the doors.

Kabul University, walled and gated, was in better shape than the rest of the city. Many old trees were still intact, and boys and girls were moving freely about the campus. I'd attended the engineering school there for a short while; the building was still standing, but very dilapidated. I saw a billboard announcing a US-sponsored program to rehab the school.

As I was taking photographs, a young boy and girl walking by asked me to take their picture. I snapped their photo as they embraced. Poignantly, the indomitable spirit of humanity and ardent emotions can manifest even under difficult circumstances. It warmed my heart for a moment, but only briefly.

Talking to people from different milieus made one thing very clear to me: life in the city in 2007 was far better than under the dreaded Taliban and their immediate predecessors. Although less enthusiastic than in the early days after the fall of the Taliban, people were generally happier about getting foreign assistance from the United States, Europe, and other countries. While the International Stability Assistance Force (ISAF) was engaging the Taliban with military force, the United Nations, NGOs, and humanitarian organizations were busy with different aspects of nation-building.

However, there's much concern about warlords and the Taliban's resurgence. People's frustrations stemmed from the United States allying with uncouth warlords—for the express purpose of deposing the Taliban. This tenuous alliance gave warlords an unseemly legitimacy and unruly power in Afghan eyes. Many asked, "Why didn't the United States come in with sufficient force early on, so as not to depend on the warlords?" After all, the warlords had caused much of Kabul's destruction and had created an environment of fear and insecurity that catalyzed the Taliban's rise to power.

People close to President Hamid Karzai told me how frustrated he had become, tireless as he was in trying to bring about stability to all of Afghanistan. Some of the major underlying reasons for the instability were the warlords, Pakistan's continued undeclared support for the Taliban, rampant corruption, and opium production and smuggling. Through it all, corruption within the corridors of power was of particular concern due to its unwieldy scope and broad reach.

The influx of aid from America and other countries had trickled up and down the economy to fuel an assortment of businesses, such as firms providing security guards, restaurants, and shops selling handicrafts. The well-connected had appropriated the lion's share of foreign aid monies. Unfortunately, too, a high percentage of foreign aid to Afghanistan ended up back in donor countries in the form of contracts, salaries, and fees. For example, according to reports, Americans, South Africans, and other mercenaries working as security guards earned up to $1,000 a day. In comparison, the average salary of a teacher in Kabul was $50 per month. Sadly, Afghanistan's heavy reliance on foreign entities, along with the lack of physical infrastructure and good governance, contributed to its continued deterioration.

As I went about Kabul in April 2007, I tried to identify with the new character of the city I'd left behind thirty years ago. It hurt to feel like a stranger in the very place I'd grown up—within the embrace of a loving, extended family and good friends. Over 80 percent of my Kabuli cohorts were gone. What I saw instead were people who'd brought back with them the culture of refugee camps, scarred by the ravages of war. I'm not faulting them, as many were victims of circumstances. The Cold War and what ensued played a big hand, too.

Kabulis in the spring of 2007 were not as fortunate as those of us who'd been able to leave; instead, they'd had to endure, every day, the ruthless events of the past three decades—through no fault of their own.

The most overwhelming challenge for the government at that time, which continues today, was to provide an atmosphere where people can feel safe and secure. Furthermore, people needed to share in and benefit from the peace dividends promised to them. Only then would there be a possibility to influence people's mentalities and their actions—which are the most difficult to modify, let alone change.

However, regardless of all the despair, I saw genuine acts of kindness, respect, and acceptance. Perhaps beneath that sense of hopelessness laid glimmers of hope and optimism for the present, and the future?

Regrettably, I was only able to spend a week in Kabul at that time.

My prayers were for Afghanistan to regain its majestic splendor—and for the beautiful spirit of its people to shine forth brightly again.

Postscript to Prologue

Back home in Naples, Florida, the bittersweet experience of finally being able to see the country of my birth, a country so devastated by internecine fighting, kept gnawing at me. While continuing with my aviation consulting business, I wondered what I could do to contribute, and how effective my contribution could be, toward Afghanistan's recovery.

I returned to Kabul in July 2008. That time, I stayed five weeks. My experiences ran the gamut of "the good, the bad, and the ugly." I visited the presidential palace twice, for the first-year anniversary of King Zahir Shah's passing and for the late king's son-in-law's funeral. High-level posts in government and private sectors were offered to me. I met with members of the present ruling Karzai family. One brother, Mahmoud, co-owner of Pamir Airways, offered me the CEO post; I declined as I didn't want to compromise my core values. After meeting the country's first vice president, Marshal Fahim, I couldn't wait to wash my hands! Fahim, along with other warlords, had been responsible in destroying Kabul, along with murdering and maiming countless people.

I was still mulling what to do when serendipity intervened in spring 2009. I found out about the US Department of State's USAID civilian surge program for Afghanistan. I applied and was notified in July that I would be senior adviser to a Provincial Reconstruction Team. Training followed at the Foreign Services Institute in Washington, D.C., in September and at a military civilian program in Indiana.

As frustrating as dealing with bureaucracy was, I welcomed the opportunity to serve my birth and adopted countries. Both have shaped who I am today. Giving back as best I could to both was the natural next step—rebuilding Afghanistan while engaging in one of America's most important foreign policy challenges impacting national and international security.

From October 13, 2009, to January 5, 2011, I returned to Kabul as a US State Department diplomat. I returned for a second tour of duty with the Department of Defense from March 1, 2013, to February 20, 2013.

The following are missives I penned to family and friends during my second tour.

CHAPTER 1

7.27.2011:
Tribute to Ghulam Haidar Hamidi, Mayor of Kandahar City

I worked with Ghulam Haidar Hamidi, the Mayor of Kandahar City, day in and day out from October 2009 to January 2011. I became his de facto mentor, but, more accurately, I was his facilitator and co-partner in matters of good governance and his dealings with the Kandahar Provincial Reconstruction Team (KPRT).

While serving as a US State Department peace diplomat in Kandahar City from October 13, 2009, to January 5, 2011 (which I covered in *Sardar: From Afghanistan's Golden Age to Carnage*), my job was to parlay American culture and politics within the Afghan context to help reintroduce peaceful rule of law back into Afghanistan.

Mayor Hamidi lived for close to twenty years within the sheltered environs of northern Virginia where Afghan refugees had encamped. However, he returned to serve Kandahar City at President Hamid Karzai's behest.

I served as a bridge for him between these two worlds—in gently explaining politics, bureaucratic policies, and the complexities of USAID procedures and military funded projects. I also mediated between him and the KPRT when disagreements relative to the city's projects and other matters arose. Due to his confidence in me, but, more importantly, due to his extraordinary generosity, Hamidi always accepted my suggestions and recommendations to break any impasse we faced.

Although I'd previously known the Mayor (or "Haidar Jan" as I addressed him respectfully), I got to know his noble mettle during my time working with him. He was a true patriot—honest, indefatigable, courageous, kindhearted, and refreshingly outspoken. He was under constant pressure from his family to leave Kandahar City as they feared for his life, but he stubbornly refused. He believed that, when his time came, he'd depart the world arena satisfied in having pursued his life's mission with integrity.

When Ahmad Wali Karzai (President Hamid Karzai's younger brother) was assassinated on July 12, 2011, I called Mayor Hamidi to gauge his reaction and urged him to be careful. His reply was, "Today, it was Ahmad Wali, another day will be mine." He said we'd return to the heavenly fields sooner or later; that it shouldn't deter us from doing our jobs as best we could. Unbeknownst to him, his life, too, would be taken two weeks after he spoke those fatal words!

While the Taliban claimed responsibility for his murder, it is unknown who was responsible. Haidar Jan had made many enemies by challenging the culture of impunity that was reigning supreme in Kandahar City.

Mayor Hamidi took on warlords and powerbrokers who had illegally and forcefully taken over public lands and properties. He collected taxes and revenues such as rents from municipality-owned properties. One of my first assignments in late 2009 at KPRT was to audit the city's revenues. I found that Mayor Hamidi had increased revenues seven-fold in less than three years—from 30 million to 220 million Afghanis, with very limited resources available to him.

In summer 2010, Mayor Hamidi made headlines for evicting people from a government-owned property the Mazali brothers had usurped and taken over for their marketplace. The site was razed, and Taimur Shahi School was built with Canadian funding.

In 2010, two deputy mayors of Kandahar City were assassinated. Lower-ranking municipal workers also lost their lives, while many others were threatened. Hamidi attributed these brutal assaults on his municipality to his even-handed effectiveness in governing a city of outlaws.

Mayor Hamidi's friendship with the Karzai family went back six decades. But, he disavowed favors to them. I once saw Hamidi hang up on Ahmad Wali Karzai because he wanted Hamidi to allow a person with religious-political connections in Kabul to install a phone transmission tower on his city property.

Gul Agha Shezai, former Governor of Kandahar, sold several thousand acres of public land east of Kandahar City to a group of developers for a gated community. The most prominent group member was Mahmood Karzai, an older Karzai. After assuming mayoral responsibilities, Hamidi abrogated the contract when he found out the public land had been sold very cheaply, at $300 per "jereeb" (a half acre). By then, the Aino Mina gated community was built and expanding. Hamidi single-handedly renegotiated the sale with a legally binding contract that increased prices retroactively to $3,000 per jereeb, resulting in a ten-fold increase for city coffers (regardless of the developers' influential connections).

Losing Mayor Hamidi on July 27, 2011, wasn't just personally devastating. It was heartbreaking for Afghanistan and the international community's efforts to stabilize Kandahar and the restive south. If there's any hope of rebuilding economic and sociopolitical capacity so that self-sustaining governance can be returned to a secure, stable Afghanistan, it will require the service of patriotic souls like Mayor Hamidi—without taking their lives in return.

It's unconscionable and pathetic we spend billions on Afghanistan, but can't pay for better security to protect Afghan officials whose services are vital for our transition plans.

CHAPTER 2

3. 12. 2012:
My Second Deployment as a GS-15 Civilian

Warning: This missive is a very detailed account of my travel to and work in Afghanistan. My aim is to convey a sense of what it takes to deploy to a theater of operations through the Department of Defense (DOD) and the challenges facing a civilian in doing so.

My second deployment to Afghanistan started at the sprawling Fort Benning Army Base, straddling the Georgia-Alabama border. I arrived at the Columbus, Georgia, airport on the morning of March 1, 2012. A couple of enlisted men, a sergeant, a lieutenant colonel (LTC), and I were driven to base in a white school bus shuttle, arriving there an hour later. The first stop was to drop off the soldiers. The rest of us who were Afghanistan-bound were taken to a special facility for deployment personnel.

The bus driver told us to take our gear to the billeting office. I struggled with my two heavy bags weighing over 150 pounds. Fortunately, the facility had wheeled carts that made it easier. Others were carrying as much stuff, too. The billeting people gave me a blanket, a pair of sheets, a pillow case, and a room assignment. I pulled my heavy cart uphill to the building, but couldn't get in because I didn't have the combination to the lock. Darn! Darn!!

And, just as luck would have it, the skies opened up right then. Cursing profusely, I went back down the hill to the billeting office for the code. To my surprise, it wasn't the single room I was entitled to, given my civilian rank that's equivalent to a colonel. But, I decided not to spend more energy over it. (A good decision because I didn't have roomies after all.)

RETURN TO KABUL

I was a member of AfPak Hands, created by the Department of Defense, which began in 2009. This program recruited officers up to the rank of colonel and some noncommissioned officers to commit about three years of their careers serving in Afghanistan and Pakistan. Recruits were immersed in intensive training in one of two Afghan languages, Dari or Pashto. Dari is the same as Farsi, which is spoken in Iran, but with different accents (similar to English being spoken in different accents by the Brits and us). Pashto is the majority tongue and lingua franca of the Pashtunistan area, which is controlled by Pakistan. After initial language and cultural training, cohorts deployed to Afghanistan to be embedded in various Afghan agencies as mentors and facilitators, thereby increasing Afghan capacity. After a year's tour, members were replaced by previous Hands to provide continuity. They spent one year back in the United States at their units and then were rotated back to Afghanistan. I was one of very few civilians in this program. In our cohort 3B, I was the only civilian among thirty people.

We gathered in a huge hanger-like building for deployment instructions. There were 120 of us, mostly destined for Afghanistan, but also to Kuwait, Iraq, and other points. Luggage tags lay on tables with instructions on marking them up. A sergeant gave me additional tags with "DV" on them for colonels and above, for military brass and civilians. DV means "Distinguished Visitor." I thought this designation might entitle me to a baggage handler, thus freeing me from the burden of carrying my heavy loads and perhaps a few more perks. But I soon realized it was wishful thinking!

Next morning, I got up at 5:30 a.m. I brought my luggage to a specific area for AfPak Hands. We lined up bags according to a military procedure and were herded back into the big hall. Military people carrying guns rendered their weapons inoperable by threading a plastic cord through the magazine and chamber. Long guns were locked up in special cases. We went through another room where everyone was wanded to ensure nothing would jeopardize flight safety. Then we were sequestered back inside the big hall. We ate lunch around 11:30 a.m. We were separated into groups and instructed to board busses taking us to the flight line. I was in the first group and third to board (nice to be a DV) an old Boeing 767-300ER belonging to Omni Air International. The entire aircraft configuration was coach. I took the bulkhead first row with no one next to me.

We departed Fort Benning at 2:00 p.m. for Shannon, Ireland. The crew was all Americans. The food was disgusting. Seven plus hours later, we landed in Shannon. The command sergeant major announced a layover of two hours for the aircraft to refuel. Military rule barred us from drinking even one beer. The restaurant-bar was open at 2:00 a.m. I had smoked salmon with my favorite Irish whole wheat soda bread.

While hanging out in the lounge, a burly American introduced himself as the military attaché. Others immediately disliked him, wondering how he got a cushy job and didn't have to put his life in danger. He said the flight to Kuwait would be delayed due to air traffic problems at the destination. Sandwiches, soft drinks, other junk food, and coffee were ordered for us. We waited some more and finally, after four hours, boarded the plane.

We landed over six hours later at Ali Al Salem Air Base, twenty-three miles from the Iraqi border; this base is shared with the United States and Kuwait. The command sergeant major announced everyone was to remain seated and to let the DVs deplane first.

It paid to be a DV! We boarded busses, but no sooner had I boarded, than a military captain asked if there were any DVs among the passengers. I identified myself. He said, "Come with me, sir." I followed him to a waiting van and he drove me to the base ahead of others. I registered, went over to transient billeting where they assigned me a tent and received clean sheets and a blanket. The others arrived an hour later.

More instructions were provided relative to our departure from Kuwait to Kabul. AfPak Hands were separated from others. The next morning, we went to a designated place with our luggage where we waited for more instructions. We loaded our bags onto two pallets, secured with netting, plastic sheets, and straps to keep them dry. Two busses took us to the flight line to a C130 military transport plane. The C130 had two rows of seats, made of very uncomfortable canvas material, on each side facing the middle. It had one large open compartment shared by people and cargo, so both luggage pallets were loaded on after we took our seats.

The main pilot, a US Air Force captain, came down to ask the two flight crew members whether everything was in order for takeoff. A few minutes later, the engines roared, the props began whirling, and the plane taxied for takeoff. The C130 aircraft doesn't have lavatories. Instead, it has a "piss tube" in the rear left side, with a piece of canvas attached to the wall for partial privacy. We had taken packages of MRE (meals ready to eat) and bottled water with us. I limited my water intake to avoid the piss tube. Between unyielding canvas seats, stiff knees, and the protruding feet of people across from me, I had to get up forty-five minutes into the flight. I found a place up front and stood there the rest of the flight.

Our first stop was ISAF Joint Command (IJC) Headquarters, located at the Kabul International Airport (KAIA), where we stayed a few days. KAIA is jointly used by military and commercial flights. Our approach and landing was an unforgettable adventure. The aircraft swayed violently from side to side, up and down, in all directions. I was afraid someone would throw up, which would've made matters even worse. Fortunately, nothing happened. Everyone heaved a sigh of relief when the wheels safely touched the runway. We went into a small reception area to wait for our bags. The pallets were brought to the door by the waiting area. We formed a human chain to unload the pallets. While waiting, the captain came in, and we commented on the interesting landing. She very casually said she had performed an "assault landing" for practice, by pretending we were under fire and therefore needed to take evasive action.

A major and a captain responsible for coordinating AfPak Hands greeted us and briefed our travel team leader. By then, it was about 9:00 p.m. We were to get our bags and find our tents. It had snowed; it was cold and muddy; dragging luggage was a bear. When I arrived at my tent, all lower-level bunk beds were taken. I clambered up to the upper bunk bed. There was no place to store my two bags, so I hoisted up a roller bag and left the duffel on the floor (see picture in the photo gallery). There were twenty-eight of us in a tent designed for eight. Showers and latrines were forty yards away.

Military personnel regularly travel with all their gear, such as sleeping bags and cold and hot weather fatigues. But as a novice civilian, I was ill-prepared. I went to billeting to get blankets and sheets, but returned empty-handed. I found a dirty blanket and pillow under a bed and spent the night with my clothes on. The next morning, I bought a sleeping bag from the German PX.

Coordinators of AfPak Hands had organized orientation seminars and presentations, which were totally useless, in my opinion. They wanted us to be busy until we got to Camp Julien for counterinsurgency (COIN) training. We discussed where we'd be assigned. To my chagrin, I realized I was just a number; no one cared where I'd go. I told them about my background, but no one listened. I ran into General Terry, a three-star who worked with me in Kandahar, but he told me he wouldn't become IJC commander until June and that he was only there for a couple of days. Bummer! I'd been assigned to Combined Joint Interagency Task Force 435 (CJIATF 435). It includes personnel from all the branches of the US military, coalition members, Afghan army, as well as the US Departments of State and Justice, among others. It has the responsibility for the Parwan Detention Center, which houses over three thousand prisoners. Its mission consists of training and advising the Afghan National Army to develop investigation, prosecution, and other operations related to the detention of insurgents based on rule of law. The responsibility for the Parwan Detention Center would be transferred to the Afghan authorities at some point in the future. I was there to serve, so it shouldn't have made a difference, but I felt that I'd be more effective elsewhere given my background.

On March 9 we got ready to move to Camp Julien, located on the outskirts of Kabul. Again, as with everything military it was "hurry up and wait." We finally boarded two Chinook helicopters with our belongings for the ten-minute trip. It was cold; both windows of the chopper were open, manned by two gunners on each side. At camp, we found that thirty of us were to sleep in one big room. We didn't have to double up, so we used upper bunks to store our stuff. Showers and toilets were attached, so there was no need to venture out into the cold.

COIN training went on all day long, all week long. Our group included American, Afghan, German, Italian, and other coalition member officers. I didn't need any of the training, but since I was with this group, I had to follow them. It was a very useless exercise for AfPak Hands who've gone through much more rigorous training. I was very disappointed with the poor quality and irrelevance of the training to what we were there for. But, someone has to check off a box and that's the reason we went through it—as far as I can ascertain.

Camp Julien is located between two palaces, Darul Aman and Tajbeg (the Queen's Palace), both destroyed in the mid-1990s. I took some officers for a walk to the Queen's Palace. They couldn't believe Afghanistan had such splendid architectural marvels. See the photos in the photo gallery. The BBC has an audio slideshow on Tajbeg, the Queens's Palace by filmmaker John McHugh at: *http://news.bbc.co.uk/2/hi/south_asia/8589535.stm (3.29.2010)*.

It had been snowing on and off for the last couple of days. The surrounding mountains were covered with snow and beautiful—but cold. In a week's time, the group would separate to fan out. I was headed for Camp Phoenix in Kabul and had yet to find out whether I would stay there for my tour or move on elsewhere.

CHAPTER 3

3.20.2012:
The Taliban Promote a Culture of Intimidation and Corruption

I thought that I had one more week at Camp Julien. But to my disappointment we remained longer. The COIN training had ended, but they amended the program for AfPak Hands to include more language and Afghan cultural training. Incidentally, this was the last COIN training they did. It had finally dawned on someone that we'd entered the transition phase for Afghanistan to take on more responsibility for its own security. Therefore, these scenarios taken from various military campaigns were no longer relevant to the current situation. Even my military colleagues expressed exasperation at COIN's lack of usefulness. They had the same feeling about the language and cultural training, too. After the first class, they told me the training they went through in the States before deployment was much more in-depth.

For language classes, DOD flew in four instructors (Afghan Americans) all the way from the Defense Language Institute in Monterey, California, for three days of classes, lasting two hours a day. Was it too difficult to find language instructors locally?

I told the Hands' coordinator I didn't need the additional training. I'd have been more useful if I could have started contributing instead of wasting time there. But he couldn't make any exceptions. I decided to attend some of these sessions anyway. I was really disappointed as to the quality of the lectures and the qualifications of the lecturers. I became very disruptive as I could not help but challenge them on many points. Perhaps for an American soldier with a shallow background on Afghanistan it was adequate, but that is not an excuse for the amount of money spent on these programs. The contractor responsible for the cultural lectures on the Afghan bureaucracy was the son of General Rahim Wardak, the current Afghan minister of defense. One could wonder how he got the contract, but it is evident that he secured it through his father's connections. The culture of impunity that the powerful Afghan war profiteers have created will be very detrimental to any eventual success of this mission. At the end of the course there was a lavish dinner that the contractor had catered. One of the officers sitting next to me said that this was one of the best dinners he had ever had. I told him that he should eat as much as he could because we had all paid for the dinner by way of tax dollars!

I stayed at Julien until March 23. Our tax dollars at work! It was apparent they weren't prepared to receive me purposefully, so they were buying time.

Incidents such as the killing of civilians in Kandahar by a rogue soldier and the burning of Qurans at the Parwan Detention Center under US watch added to our challenges. On Sunday, March 11, soon after the news of the civilian killings broke, I called the Governor of Kandahar. Details were sketchy and he was very distraught. He said no sooner had we taken a step forward, than we're forced to go back twenty steps. The killing of sixteen people was tragic enough, but it couldn't have come at a worst moment. There was already much apprehension among people as to what the future would portend after our departure. More insidiously, such events were exploited by insurgents actively supported by Pakistan.

Many violent demonstrations, which periodically took place and were reported by the media, were not spontaneous reactions of aggrieved Afghans. Rather, there's ample evidence they were organized by none other than Gulbudeen Hekmatyar. We supported Hekmatyar during the Soviet occupation of Afghanistan, but he turned against US and Afghan interests. He and his murderous group continued to be harbored and supported by the Pakistanis, but at times, he also received support and shelter from Iran.

Although Afghans weren't happy with the results of our efforts, they didn't want us to leave in haste. What was heard in the press was propaganda spun by the Taliban and other Pakistani proxy groups (with the support and encouragement of Pakistan's government) to influence American public opinion. They're smart about attention-grabbing headlines having a profound effect in swaying public opinion. They're convinced, and rightfully so, that an erosion of American (and other international) public support would hasten a self-fulfilling prophecy. Our leaving prematurely would pave the way for insurgents to use Afghanistan as a breeding ground for even more extremist activities.

A cornerstone of US efforts to stabilize Afghanistan was the Village Stability Operations (VSO) program conducted by the military all over Afghanistan with the aim of working with villagers to help fend off insurgent encroachments. One tool was the Afghan Local Police, which is staffed by villagers and paid for by the Afghan government. Unfortunately, the killing of civilians in Kandahar by a member of the military VSO jeopardized this program. Karzai and others called for an end to this program and demanded we get out of the villages. Tactical errors have profound strategic consequences, of which we had to be very careful. This, obviously, was a case where a rogue soldier was solely responsible, but there were other instances where we didn't pay enough attention to avoiding tactical errors.

The fear among those who see the "Afghan problem" within a regional context is for the return of a chaotic Afghanistan reminiscent of the 1990s, which would have profound implications beyond Afghan borders, not to mention the continued suffering of Afghans. Announcing our withdrawal from Afghanistan created much confusion among the people and within government circles. It forced Afghans into a state of uneasy survival; ergo strong reactions and pronouncements were heard from Afghan lawmakers, government officials, and President Karzai. We unfortunately fell into a vicious cycle compounded by unfortunate events hurtling us into even more troubled waters.

Both Afghans and the international community needed to show bold leadership to break this cycle of mistrust and fear. Only then could everyone work together toward a sound, feasible plan for the gradual transitioning and easing of responsibilities back to Afghans.

In the short time I had been there after a year's absence, I already had the impression Afghans were not yet ready to take on full responsibility for their *own security issues. This was because corruption persisted unabated, which no one seemed to have the courage and the ability to tackle. The flight of financial capital from the country was also staggering! Estimated at $10 to $12 million daily, mostly of bills stuffed into suitcases, monies were flown out from Kabul International Airport by carriers (some of these were high-level government employees). The money went to Dubai; where it ended up thereafter was difficult to ascertain. One thing our Treasury could have done was pressure the United Arab Emirates (of which Dubai is a member country) to stop such money-laundering activities. Sources banking this "capital flight" came from international community funds for Afghanistan's reconstruction, drug trafficking, and businesses that didn't pay taxes, including siphoning off profits.*

While Afghanistan had become the world's largest opium-producing country, it's an annual $68 billion international narco-business run by international cartels. (Opium makes heroin.) The Taliban encouraged the cultivation and safe passage of opium. Afghans were not immune to the ill effects of abundant opium, either. There were an estimated 1.5 to 2 million addicts or "podaries" (from the term "powder," for using the drug this way) in Afghanistan. With a lack of shelters, many Kabuli podaries perished in the harsh winter of 2011–2012.

There was some good news on the drug front, though. The narcotics court was making progress, albeit at a snail's pace (but who knew how sustainable it would prove to be). A famous drug leader was convicted and sentenced to twenty years. With US help, the Ministry of Defense identified fifty-four areas of corruption to fix. The United States and its coalition would be doing the same with the Ministry of Interior and other government agencies. Again, how successful these efforts would be was unknown.

Corruption was deep-seated. We tried to work with the government to identify good people to diminish this problem, to the level that it wouldn't be fatal to the Afghan government.

Our kinetic operations a few months before along the Afghan-Pakistan border resulted in killing about two dozen Pakistani soldiers. This, combined with the embarrassment of eliminating Osama bin Laden under the Pakistanis' military nose, plunged our already tenuous relationship with Pakistan to a new *low. As a result, Pakistan closed our supply route from the seaport of Karachi overland through the Khyber Pass to Afghanistan. We were then forced to fly in supplies from Dubai and former Soviet Republics in the north. According to estimates, the cost of bringing in a standard container through Dubai was $130,000; it cost $30,000 for the same container from the north. But, we had only paid $9,000 through Pakistan. For this and other more important reasons, we had to rely on, and deal with, Pakistan. But it became increasingly difficult. The Pakistani military-religious complex continued to support insurgents while denying that they're doing it.*

One of our most effective ways of dealing with the bad guys was via drones. On March 20 (after the border accident), a Pakistani commission called the United States to cease drone operations inside Pakistan, and to apologize. It remained to be seen whether and when Pakistan would reopen its supply routes; at the very least, Pakistan would demand more money.

At Camp Julien, we had a warming trend weather-wise, but on March 19 a strange, blinding dust storm mixed with a cold front. Visibility was very poor; even the surrounding mountains became invisible. I don't recall any kind of dust storm while growing up in Kabul in the sixties and early seventies. The sky was always blue during the day and full of flickering stars at night. Thirty years of war had completely denuded Kabul of its trees, gardens, and greenery. The city had grown exponentially and sprawled out at least eight-fold. Shanty neighborhoods had sprung up without any kind of sensible planning and infrastructure support. Consequently, Kabul had been transformed into a dust bowl. Rain and snow cleared the air a bit, but the mountains promoted air pollution. On that day, the winds died down and visibility became slightly better. Snow on nearby mountains, however, looked gray with remnants of the dust storm settling over them.

My hope was that once I got out of Camp Julien and started work, I would have more interesting things to write about. But in the meantime, I had to vent!

CHAPTER 4

4.3.2012:
Stalled by Military Bureaucracy

We were ready on March 23 to leave Camp Julien when I got word that two people, LTC Hank Weede and I, would have to stay one more day. This was because a one-star general acting for the commander of CJIATF 435 (a three-star) decided to curtail ground movement due to a threat. In the meantime, others with different assignments in Kabul were picked up by their people. Why rules within the same war machinery operate differently for different people was beyond comprehension; my hope was to figure out these complex military puzzles by the end of my tour.

Bagram Military Air Base was a staging place to final destinations. The majority of my cohorts were assigned to the provinces. At 9:00 a.m., they boarded a huge military truck to go to the helipad less than half a mile away. Choppers arrived, but a staff sergeant decided the flight manifest was not in order. The helicopters, rotors whirling, took off without passengers. Then twenty officers were taken to a holding area, an empty cold room in the vicinity of the pad. Were they livid! Word was, they were to wait till midnight to be picked up. Although upset about having to wait another day, I was very happy I wasn't in that situation. I went to the gym, took a hot shower, and ate hot lunch and dinner instead of MRE.

During my Camp Julien stay, I got to know Afghans who had various jobs at the chow hall. Similar to my experiences at Camp Nathan Smith, when I worked at Kandahar Provincial Reconstruction Team (KPRT), they thought I was Indian (from India). I asked how they arrived at that conclusion. "You're much darker than normal Afghans," they replied. I tried explaining that I'd lived in Florida for decades and being fond of the outdoors, indulged in swimming, tennis, and other sports under the blazing sun; hence my darker skin. They couldn't grasp it. I simplified it by saying I worked outside all the time, hence my deep, dark tan.

Before leaving Camp Julien, we went to an Afghan National Army shooting range. I had chosen not to carry a weapon, but my colleagues offered me theirs to practice with. My excitement of doing some shooting was dashed when a young lieutenant in charge of the event told me I couldn't shoot. I waited more than two hours for the others to finish. Again, a total waste of time!

Military camps have very strict rules, such as armed persons entering base should clear their weapons at the entrance to avoid accidental discharges, which might kill someone or cause material damages. Loaded weapons are discharged harmlessly into sand-filled clearing barrels.

I was in the barracks one day when I heard a bang outside our door. It turned out to be an officer's sidearm going off when he attempted to clear it. This very embarrassed officer apologized profusely. Although no one was hurt and no property damage resulted, a negligent or accidental discharge is a very serious matter, which could possibly adversely affect a person's military career and/or result in that person being sent home.

An immediate investigation was launched with findings sent up the chain of command. High-ranking officers in our cohort (including me) sprang into action and wrote testimonials on the officer's behalf. Luckily for him, the deciding general issued a letter of reprimand, which remained in his file for only one year while he was in Afghanistan. Provided he didn't get himself into trouble again, after the letter was removed, his career would be unaffected. I recounted a previous similar situation at Camp Nathan Smith in my first volume, *Sardar*. In that case, the negligence of the Canadian general, Daniel Menard, was more egregious. He was subsequently tried, demoted to the rank of colonel, and forced to retire from the Canadian army. Menard's problem of negligent discharge was compounded by his liaison dangereuse with a female subordinate officer. The retired colonel Menard later came back to Afghanistan as a civilian contractor, earning a lot more money than when he was a general. The revolving door in Afghanistan serves connected people well.

With only two of us left in a room that had accommodated over thirty men until earlier today, we took turns watching our stuff. When I went to the gym, LTC Weede stayed. I reciprocated when he went to eat.

Finally, a cryptic e-mail perked me up. It stated that we'd be picked up in fifty minutes. Although it took over an hour, they finally showed up. There were two armored SUVs, an LTC, one lieutenant, and two sergeants. They loaded up our gear, and we were finally off to Camp Phoenix, the headquarters for the CJIATF 435!

We took the old Darullaman Road, now twice as wide, but devoid of the huge trees that flanked the road thirty-six years ago. I tried to see as much as I could through the tinted glass in the rainy darkness. We went past the Russian embassy with its sprawling compound and my old high school, Habibia, which brought back poignant memories.

We drove along Kabul River through downtown, making our way to Wazir Akbar Khan district, and finally to Jalalabad Road on which Camp Phoenix is located. Jalalabad Road is the main artery connecting Kabul to the city of Jalalabad in the east and to Pakistan's border leading to the infamous Khyber Pass. During my youth, we spent winters in Jalalabad because of its warm, inviting climate. It is only about a hundred miles from Kabul, but the climate is warm enough for citrus fruit trees to grow. While Kabul sits on a plateau 6,000 feet above sea level, Jalalabad's elevation is about 1,900 feet, explaining its marked climatic difference from Kabul. The city was used as a winter capital by King Habibullah and his son, King Amanullah. Many in the military, but also diplomats at the US Embassy refer to Jalalabad as J-bad. Jalalabad refers to the name of its modern founder, Jalal, in the sixteenth century. J-bad means nothing, but we are very impatient to try to relate and understand the places and the people we want to help. No wonder why our efforts sometimes fall short!

Upon arrival, we got sheets, blankets, and keys to our rooms, which were much smaller than walk-in closets at home. Community showers and toilets were at the end of the hall.

CJIATF 435, where I worked, was commanded by a three-star general, Keith Huber. My immediate boss was Rear Admiral Judge Advocate General Crawford, assisted by Colonel Ben Klappe of the Netherlands as chief of staff and Colonel Soren Knudsen of the Danish army as deputy commander. The next morning, I went to the office around eight, but no one knew what to do with me. I insisted on seeing Rear Admiral Crawford. He asked for my resume and told me to return at noon; whereupon, he told me to take a couple more days to settle in while he pondered my assignment. I was so anxious to start, only to be disappointed yet again!

In the meantime, Colonel Klappe dropped in. He'd seen my resume; with my technical background, I could do project management, he said. I countered that everybody could do project management, but very few people have my skills relevant to Afghanistan's needs.

The following morning, he came by again with my assignment for at least the next month. Project management! The first project would assess forensics laboratories and their capabilities in Afghanistan. I would be travelling to various parts of the country to review these labs and formulate recommendations. Ha! The Afghan police couldn't even properly handle a crime scene, let alone engage in sophisticated evidence analysis.

I was sent what had already been done. I then sent my proposal to J3 (the military designation for operations organization) team chiefs around the country. Based on their input, I would go on a fact-finding tour. Nothing moves fast through the military chain of command.

On Friday, March 30, I was finally able to go to our embassy to see Mimi Gregory of the Naples Council on World Affairs, who was invited to Kabul by Ambassador Ryan Crocker. I'd failed in my first two attempts on the twenty-seventh and twenty-eighth due to last-minute security concerns en route. The embassy is only a few miles from Camp Phoenix.

I had lively discussions over lunch with Mimi and members of her group. We indulged in hamburgers from the grill outside the dining facility (DFAC) by the pool. You've had well-done burgers, but these were done to death. DFAC contractors more than overcook everything to make sure no one gets sick from food borne micro-organisms in the short run. But, they don't care about feeding people food devoid of any nutrition, which causes health problems later on.

Mimi invited me to go shopping with her group and Ambassador Crocker. A few minutes later, we met by the building where the ambassador's apartment was. I knew about it because I'd been invited there by our former ambassador, Karl Eikenberry.

Off we went to the bazaar located past the HQ ISAF, adjacent to the embassy. It's similar to a flea market with over a hundred makeshift shacks and stands. You can find everything from jewelry to Afghan carpets, from knockoff antiques to perfumes and sunglasses. One person even offered prescription glasses with transition lenses, and others offered cheap Chinese electronics, pirated movies, and all kinds of junk imported from India, Pakistan, and other places.

Our party got busy shopping. I was impressed by the ambassador's haggling prowess, which he must've honed through years of foreign service in exotic locales. He bought a number of items, and he knew many of the vendors. I guess that's how one learns bazaar diplomacy, which can come in very handy in Afghanistan, Iraq, and Pakistan (where he had also served as ambassador previously).

I really wanted to talk to him. Mimi tried pushing for it, too, but we couldn't get his attention. I was running out of time and said goodbye; he thanked me for my service.

On April 2, I was going to meet staff at the central forensics lab at the Ministry of Interior. Two American officers were killed there a month before in a so called "green-on-blue" attack. Afghan soldiers wear green uniforms, so any insider attack on coalition members by their Afghan partners is termed green-on-blue. There had been a worrisome increase of this type of attack on the international coalition members. We were trying to accelerate the training of Afghan security forces, but distrust between the two parties might have had an ill effect. My trip was canceled because the Admiral had to go somewhere else. It was logistically impossible to support my trip, too. Due to security measures instituted after the officers' murders, I had to be accompanied by an armed escort (guardian angels) when

I visited Afghan bureaucracies. There weren't enough assets to carry out the mission (and follow military procedures). It was frustrating not having enough assets to do the right things in Afghanistan while invading Iraq at the same time. When the decision was made to invade Iraq, the situation in Afghanistan went south.

Camp Phoenix was very crowded. There were several thousand people who called the place home. It was dusty, vibrant with vehicle traffic, densely dotted with tents and various buildings and structures, with an Afghan bazaar and even a PX for body massages from Filipino ladies in a dingy spa. I went to check out the massage scene, but decided to carry on with my stiff back rather than submit my body to Phoenix Spa treatments!

I started a campaign to get out of Phoenix. I hoped to succeed before I completely lost my patience. I could survive in bad conditions provided I could contribute. Judging from my initial experience of not being gainfully employed, it would have been a total waste to stay there under those conditions. When nothing's sure, everything's possible!

CHAPTER 5

4.19.2012:
Revisiting Camp Nathan Smith and Kandahar Province

Fortunately my campaign to get a different job paid off. My new assignment was at HQ ISAF, adjacent to the US Embassy in the Green Zone and close to the presidential palace in Kabul.

I was assigned to the Red Team, an internal think tank tasked with presenting different and opposing views. A brainchild of General Petraeus, who wanted to ensure that self-actualization and validation of team mentality wouldn't adversely affect policy, Red Team got information from various sources to analyze, including viewpoints from insurgents.

US Navy Captain Heidi Berg was team director. (A navy captain is equivalent to an army colonel in rank.) I had lunch and a long conversation with her deputy, Nigel Little, a former Australian professor of history and met an Iranian American army captain and others on my team. It wasn't exactly what I wanted to do, but it was certainly better than the previous situation. I was hopeful that I could use my connections to discover as many different viewpoints as possible and help formulate policy more effectively.

People at Rule of Law Field Force Afghanistan (ROLFF-A) supported my leaving for this new post. ROLFF-A was part of the larger CJIATF 435. ROLFF-A was headed by a rear admiral. Many colonels, other assorted officers, and noncommissioned officers were enlisted there. My impression was that the entire CJIATF 435 command structure was geared toward serving the three highest-ranked people. I bounced this idea off a few officers and they agreed.

Since the command mission was to help bring justice to Afghanistan, there was a token two-star Afghan general, Marjan Shuja. In his midsixties, he had served his junior years in the Afghan army's Fourth Mechanized Armored Division in the 1970s, when the going was good. Promoted to general in the late 1980s by the communist government in Kabul, he was a recycled colonel as CJIATF 435's Afghan commander. His mentor was LTC Hank Weede, who deployed to Afghanistan with me in cohort 3B.

General Shuja and his staff attended English classes daily, drank tea, talked lots, and once in a while attended detainee release ceremonies. He was mostly ignored by his American counterparts and all but shunned by his Afghan chain of command. I talked to him a few times about the past; but he had a distorted view of history and didn't realize I grew up in Afghanistan and remember the situation well. I felt sorry for him.

CJIATF 435 was responsible for a huge detention facility controlled by the US government. The Karzai government wanted control transferred back to Afghan authorities. The agreement was recently signed; in six months, the Afghan government would be sole custodian—of a huge task. The sprawling center held over three thousand inmates; talk about "the Bad and the Ugly!" I thought I might facilitate this transition, which I'd be good at, but the people in charge didn't understand my background. Que sera, sera!

Before leaving for my new position at HQ ISAF, I took a trip back to Kandahar to assess capability there for forensics analysis to help the Afghan criminal justice system move toward an evidence-based process. At the forefront was forensics capability, which entails properly collecting and handling crime scene materials, then analyzing evidence in solving criminal cases. My mission was to interview police investigators, prosecutors, and judges and inspect facilities to ascertain capabilities.

The command's operations organization arranged this trip. At 9:00 a.m., I was escorted by three sergeants to the military part of Kabul International Airport to check in two hours before departure. I had been told we'd leave at 11:30 a.m., but I found that ISAF Flight 71 wouldn't leave until 5:30 p.m. I was very surprised because the military doesn't usually make mistakes.

Security conditions can change very suddenly. I ate lunch, checked e-mail, and hung out until 3:30 p.m. I checked in for flight departure, including climbing on a scale with body armor and bags. I went through the metal detector into a waiting room. At 5:15 p.m., we boarded a bus for the two-hundred-yard ride to board the plane.

A Transall C160 French military transport plane made the hour-and-fifteen-minute flight to Kandahar Air Field (KAF). KAF's bigger, dustier, and dirtier than the last time I saw it, with twenty-nine thousand soldiers and support personnel. I stayed in the admiral's room and had the use of his office; it was nice of them to give me such great accommodations.

I tracked down Rachel and Colin who'd worked with me at Camp Nathan Smith (CNS) and now worked at Regional Platform South. We had a good time reminiscing. My plan was to go to CNS on that Monday, but a lockdown came on after simultaneous insurgent attacks in Kabul on Sunday. I used the day to tour ISAF's forensics lab. The navy lieutenant in charge gave me a two-hour tour of a world-class facility, complete with DNA analysis capabilities and the whole enchilada, primarily used for identifying and arresting terrorists who make and set off Improvised Explosive Devices (IEDs).

The next day, I went to Maiwand Police Zone Headquarters, located outside KAF and thus unaffected by the lockdown. I met with Colonel Rahmatullah Sidiqi, head of the Criminal Investigation Division for this zone, which includes Kandahar and two other southern provinces, Zabul and Oruzgan. It turned out that he was from Arghandab Valley and belonged to the Mohammadzai tribe, too. I had accidentally stumbled onto yet another long-lost cousin. At this rate, in a couple of years, I'll become tribal chief and powerbroker in charge of a fiefdom!

Colonel Sidiqi was delighted to meet with me. He gave me a detailed tour, pointing out the forty-five-hundred-square-foot building slated for forensic activities. His American mentor, LTC Czar, was really surprised at the VIP treatment Colonel Sidiqi showed me. Later that day, the lockdown was lifted, which meant I could continue on to CNS.

We left KAF on Wednesday morning in a convoy of four Mine Resistant Ambush Protected (MRAP) vehicles. We dropped off an officer on our first stop, in Daman district. Our next stop was at Camp Nathan Smith, my former home. I was very surprised to find Alan Hanson, my Canadian deputy, and another Canadian, Philip Lupul, also there for a couple of days. The Canadians, including the three thousand military and all the forty-plus civilians had left Kandahar last year. There were only four people left over from my KPRT days who were still there, and two of them were on R&R.

Afghan staff enthusiastically greeted me, as did the barber. I asked about his older brother, who also worked at CNS, and learned that he'd immigrated to Canada with his family. A few officers who'd participated in one of my Afghanistan presentations last year also recognized me. That afternoon, we went to the courthouse in downtown Kandahar City to meet Chief Judge Himat, who was happy to see me again. I asked him about the use of forensics as evidence in trials. He was very enthused and lectured about its importance.

That evening, I was invited to a meeting with State Department and USAID folks at KPRT to discuss past and present events and issues. I was surprised by the negative attitude of some, which isn't helpful for working in Afghanistan or similar challenging environments. But overall, it was a good discussion and a few of them appreciated hearing how things were during my time there just sixteen months ago.

There were more American civilians (with the US Department of State and USAID) than ever before. But the tempo was very different. Back then, the whole place was abuzz with activities. This time, offices looked cleaner and neater; perhaps the workers had more time to keep things organized. Our mission had entered the transition phase; development projects had decreased, too.

On Thursday, April 19, I went to see Governor Wesa of Kandahar. Three MRAPs from KAF with twelve soldiers arrived at 11:00 a.m. to take me to the governor's palace. The palace grounds were in full bloom with beautiful flowers; the rose bushes were especially colorful and fragrant. I arrived just before noon, but the governor was in a staff meeting. I had routinely attended his staff meetings when I worked in Kandahar. But this time, I waited patiently. I met people who thought I'd returned for another year of service. It was good to see them all again!

But I couldn't stop thinking about the huge void left by the murder of my good friend, the late Mayor Ghulam Haidar Hamidi, and of the good times we had shared. The first chapter in this book is a heartfelt tribute to him. I also thought lots about late Deputy Governor Latif Ashana, who was murdered a few months before Hamidi.

While waiting, I asked the governor's staff about Kandahar City's municipality situation and was told the number of employees had doubled due to the late Mayor's efforts to increase salaries and to enact other protective measures. He'd have been so happy to see his efforts paying off for the people of the city he loved so much and for whom he gave his life!

The governor invited me to have lunch with him and his wife, Rangina Wesa, in the palace's living quarters. Dr. Rangina Wesa is an obstetrician-gynecologist who received her medical degree from Kabul University in the late 1970s. She returned with her husband from Vancouver, Canada. She supports women and education issues in Kandahar. We had a wonderful lunch. Despite setbacks such as the killing of seventeen locals at the hands of one of our soldiers and other war horrors, there had also been good progress. For example, Zhari, one of the districts which had been totally in the hands of insurgents, had opened several schools—including ones for girls. We talked about the forensics capabilities in greater Kandahar and other matters. Governor Wesa reassured me of his full support for future projects. I had to reluctantly say goodbye because I didn't want to make my escort of twelve soldiers wait any longer.

The trip back to KAF took forty minutes. I kept thinking about my short and bittersweet visit to the city in which I'd spent sixteen months just over a year before.

RETURN TO KABUL

I woke up early to a very rainy Friday morning to get ready for my trip back to Kabul. Sergeant Cruz drove me a mile to the flight line, where I registered and waited for ISAF 22 departing at 12:30 p.m. This time, it was a Spanish air force C130 transport plane (for people and cargo) that took me back to Kabul.

In a couple of days, I would move to HQ ISAF.

CHAPTER 6

5.13.2012:
Three Months of DOD Deployment—with Nothing to Show for It

On Tuesday, April 24, I awoke with high anticipation to leave Camp Phoenix at 9:00 a.m. for HQ ISAF, where General John Allen, a four-star marine who replaced General Petraeus, was commander. He also commanded US forces Afghanistan.

But, just before my departure was to take place, I learned that road security conditions were "red," meaning that all movements to and from Phoenix were curtailed until further notice. I'd already brought my bags with me, and they were waiting outside as black clouds gathered overhead. But, a Good Samaritan moved them under the stairs. Around 10:00 a.m., the "red" condition was lifted, and there was a vehicle ready to leave for the US Embassy. They loaded my stuff into an armored Chevy Suburban, and off we went.

Upon my arrival at HQ ISAF, I learned that the director had asked Tony Zimmermann, a retired military officer and presently a civilian, to be my sponsor and to walk me around and help me process in. I'd no idea what a lengthy chore this would be, in dealing with ISAF. To my mind, "international" stands for more bureaucracy and red tape.

Tony took me to a tent and advised me to claim a bed, in case there'd be a problem getting sleeping quarters. Huh, I thought, I've come full circle. I was in a tent with over twenty people when I first arrived for this DOD deployment, clawed my way up to a tiny room, and ended up back in the pit again. I didn't say anything to Tony; just followed instructions. By then, it was 1:00 p.m. and lunchtime at the dining facility (DFAC). The food seemed pretty good. I commented that ISAF's DFAC was better than Phoenix's. But, I should've been accustomed to this deceiving pattern by then. The food was bad everywhere; it's just that going to a new DFAC made it seem better. It took only a day to realize the new place was as unappetizing as the rest.

After lunch, we resumed processing by going to the billeting office station manned by an Italian officer. I filled out forms and was told to come back in a couple of days. I was directed to station number two, where I met a Spanish officer responsible for billeting. He assigned me to Room 114 in the transient building and instructed me to proceed to station number 3 to get a temporary badge. At station 3, I dealt with a French officer, which went smoothly because I spoke to him in French. He gave me the temporary badge in exchange for my driver's license. We next went to a different building, to the American National Support Element, to do more paperwork. They gave me a comforter and sheets. I took the stuff to my room, where once again, the only bed available was the upper bunk. Two others were already occupying lower bunks. "Not again," I grumbled to myself, while trying to maintain my composure with Tony.

It took a week and many more office visits to finally get my badge, meal card, various computer accounts, and other sundry provisions. I attended ISAF's information systems training to bone up on procedures. Half of a Saturday was wasted listening to boring presentations about camp. I was told to go back to billeting for a permanent room assignment. I was assigned to Room 115 in the Liberty Building and found that getting there necessitated borrowing a gator to once more move my stuff. Yet again, I couldn't believe I'd have to share the room with two others; once again, the only bed was the upper bunk.

Worse, this bunk didn't have a ladder. "Dangerous gymnastics" were required to scale up and down the bed frame. I met one of my roommates who gave me the good news that the other person would be leaving in a week. Securing bed space is problematic as HQ ISAF was designed for six hundred, but the head count was up to eighteen hundred. The best I could hope for was to move to a two-person room, even though my rank made me eligible for a single.

Finally, the person below left. It was nice without a third person in the room. But, oops, I spoke too soon. Unfortunately, a new third person arrived; he bunked above me and probably hoped I'd be leaving soon. So did I!

Liberty Building was a double-storied structure built of containers with each repurposed into a room. One container on each floor was used for the bathroom. The "buildings" were constructed less than a year before, but were already falling apart. One leaked water so badly the resulting mold got it condemned. My room was on the second floor. Only one out of three showerheads was even semifunctional. Having a shower required removing the hose from the head. Still, very little water flowed out because of the leaky hose. The toilet floor reeked of foul-smelling, leaky toilets. Ugh!

I'm sure we paid vast amounts of taxpayer money to build these ISAF buildings. I wondered, if we couldn't monitor contractors to ensure we got what we paid for under our own noses, how in the world could we successfully implement development projects in areas of Afghanistan where we didn't have ready access? No wonder billions had been squandered without the desired results!

Moving on to more felicitous news, I was very enthusiastically received by the Red Team. But, I soon realized that, once again, this wasn't where I could best serve the mission. Red Team produced reams of white papers for headquarters. Analysts penned these papers for policy-making; but regardless of issues or people, they didn't have to be in Afghanistan to do this work. I hadn't come to Afghanistan to write papers on Afghanistan. My urgent desire was to use my background and expertise to bridge gaps between Afghans and Americans. Besides, if we could have solved the Afghan problem with papers, plans, and books, we wouldn't have been in the situation we were in!

HQ ISAF was very diverse. There were Germans, French, Turks, Dutch, Danes, British, Slovenians (in charge of security), many Americans, Romanians, Polish, and numerous others. I didn't understand what they all did there. I believed we could reduce staffing by at least one-third of nonessential personnel at HQ ISAF and elsewhere, such as at Camp Phoenix.

There were also lots of wasted duplicate efforts, of which Red Team was a prime example. But there were many other organizations who also justified their existence by generating reams of paperwork, holding meetings, and acting important.

I participated in a meeting with young, bright Americans at Shifafiat (which means "transparency" in English). One guy, Carl Frosberg, had written a paper on Kandahar a couple of years before when he worked for the Institute for the Study of War. The meeting was on how we could use Columbia's counterinsurgency plan as a model for Afghanistan. While there were some parallels between the two, I didn't think Afghanistan was Columbia. I asked the rhetorical question of, how about an Afghan model? We'd been there ten years and hadn't yet learned anything about developing a suitable model!

One bright guy shot back, asking what an Afghan model was. "There's no Afghan model," he insisted. I told him to read up on Afghanistan's Golden Age, between 1930 and 1973. Afghanistan then was stable and viable with security, governance, rule of law, and progress being made with socioeconomic development. And, by the way, various tribes and ethnic groups had coexisted amicably under the rule of King Zahir Shah. What kept them together? That's the $64 million question we needed to ask and explore, I emphasized.

HQ ISAF was also interesting because it was at the crossroads of Washington's Afghanistan pundits and experts. I ran into former ambassador to Afghanistan Ron Neumann and Michael O'Hanlon. Ambassador Neumann wanted to pick my brain at breakfast. A few days before, I had seen Fred and Kimberly Kagan. They, as well as many others, traveled there a few times a year to stay current, relevant, and marketable on the current affairs television/radio/lecture circuit.

The week before, I had gone "out of the wire" for the first time to visit the Commander of the Afghan National Civil Order Police (ANCOP). My boss (US Navy Captain Heidi Berg) and I were in a vehicle with an armed soldier-driver and another guard. Two colleagues, Tony and Jorge, were in another armored SUV. A third vehicle carried armed guards. We went past some familiar scenes such as my mother's commercial property across the street from Kabul City Hall and the Ministry of Education. It took about fifteen minutes to get to ANCOP Headquarters, facing Kabul Zoo.

ABDULLAH SHARIF

Marjan Defines Afghanistan's Sovereign Spirit

As a result of factional wars, Kabul Zoo was destroyed in the 1990s. A famous lion, Marjan (whose name means "precious stone"), was a gift from Germany's Cologne Zoo. Miraculously, and precariously, he survived and witnessed the destruction of Kabul and his zoo. In 1993, a foolhardy soldier showed off his "bravery" by entering the proverbial lion's den. He stroked Marjan's lioness, Chucha, who ignored him. But, Marjan couldn't stand the brazen molestation of his lioness and mauled him to death. The next day, a brother of this man took revenge by throwing a grenade or two into the lion's den. Marjan was badly injured and blinded, but he survived. The Taliban reportedly tormented the handful of animals still in the zoo when they drove the warring factions away from Kabul. But, they stopped their cruelty when they realized their actions were un-Islamic because the Prophet Muhammad loved animals.

Chucha died in 2000. A grief-stricken Marjan stopped eating for a week. The situation at the zoo deteriorated further at the onset of the US intervention in 2001. Zoo personnel went unpaid, and there was no money to buy meat for Marjan. A local butcher stepped in to provide enough meat for Marjan to survive. The story of Marjan made headlines toward the end of 2001, and donations poured in. But, it was too late. Despite veterinarian intervention, Marjan died on the morning of January 26, 2002. He was twenty-five.

As we pulled into ANCOP headquarters, memories stabbed at my consciousness as I conversed with Heidi and the Afghan guards at the gate. This used to be a prison for many years, but there was no sign of it then. The buildings were all new.

At General Zamarai Paykan's suite, we took our seats along with his French mentor Colonel Kim. The general started talking and went on talking. He was impressive and said everything we wanted to hear—he was well coached by his French handlers. Precisely at noon, we went to the adjacent room serving as both dining room and bedroom; lunch was good. We continued our talks. He was very critical of the Minister of Defense and his deputy for not doing enough. It was all about him and how he'd do things right. I was very surprised at how he controlled the whole show. He deprived us of any opportunity to ask probing questions about his claims. At the end, he desperately looked around for something to give Heidi and found a green scarf, which he personally draped over her shoulders.

Back at HQ ISAF, I made plans to move once again, because Red Team wasn't a good fit. I was there to use my background and language skills to be a bridge between Afghans and Americans. Folks at Red Team spent their time in front of computer screens and keyboards regurgitating what had already been published. It was such a waste for the mission and for me to spend my time there. I talked to people who realized my potential and were interested in my joining their organizations. One of them was involved in reintegration and reconciliation; the other was outreach to civil society and how to help rebuild it. I waited to see what would happen!

In the meantime, some scary news arrived. I had gone to Kandahar to see the governor on April 19. Exactly to the hour and minute, one week later, two assailants penetrated his security cordon to kill him. One reached his office and was killed near the couch I was sitting on when I met with Governor Wesa. The governor survived by fleeing through a back door leading to another room and locking the door behind him. I talked to him several times afterward; the attack really shook him up. It is incredible how timely actions and fortuitous presence in space determine our fates.

It was hard to believe that three months had melted off—with nothing to show for them!

CHAPTER 7

6.2.2012:
Why is Promoting Peace Such a Pipe Dream?

Thursday, May 31 was to be my last day with Red Team. I had a new assignment with Force Reintegration Cell (FRI-C). FRIC-C's efforts help the Afghan government with its peace process. The Afghan Peace and Reconciliation Program (APRP), financed by the international community to the tune of $150 million, was launched in 2010 upon the establishment of the Afghan High Peace Council (HPC). The US government contributed another $50 million. HPC included people from the country's diverse ethnic and tribal groups.

President Karzai appointed Burhanudin Rabbani as HPC chair in 2010. Chairman Rabbani had briefly served as Afghanistan's president after the fall of the Soviet-backed government in the early 1990s. The peace effort was kicked off in Kandahar in December 2010 during my last days there. I was thus able to meet Rabbani and his number two, Masoom Stanakzai, who was in charge of the Joint Secretariat (JS), HPC's operations arm, at that time.

The program started slowly, suffering bumps along the way. The most serious was the assassination of HPC Chairman Burhanudin Rabbani in September 2011. A suicide bomber claimed he had a very important message for Rabbani—then set off a bomb hidden in his turban, killing Rabbani and wounding Stanakzai. After months of indecision, Karzai appointed Rabbani's son, Salahudin, to chair HPC in April 2012. We didn't know how Salahudin would effectively push through this national peace program.

In another setback, former Talib Arsallah Rohani, who was appointed by Karzai to HPC, as well as a member of the upper house of parliament, Meshrano Jirga, were gunned down in May 2012 near Rohani's home as he was being driven to work. Karzai also appointed Rohani's son to HPC for political continuity's sake.

A major problem facing HPC was that its members were mostly former warlords, who carried notorious baggage from past killings and other atrocities. Therefore, their credibility was very much suspect. Their presence also generated speculation that HPC was a political tool for Karzai, rather than a serious mechanism to bring people into a peaceful national fold.

Many Afghan officials had misgivings about the peace process as they were convinced the Taliban were not interested in peace and were taking advantage by stalling negotiations to wait out the international community. While some Taliban may have been engaging in this tactic, APRP was geared toward foot soldiers and middle commanders without strong ideological motives, those who'd crossed the line due to other grievances or were simply tired of fighting.

The most important aspect of APRP was its community base, with local implementation in provinces and districts. It didn't provide cash for reintegration, unlike other unsuccessful former programs. Those reintegrating were required to (1) renounce violence, (2) give up arms, (3) undergo biometric registration, and (4) be accepted by their communities. They were then eligible for a six-month stipend until they could provide for themselves.

This program also funded small projects aimed at community recovery. Recruits would eventually be eligible for recruitment by Afghan National Security Forces such as the Afghan National Police and the Afghan National Army.

Although program pace varied region to region, over four thousand fighters had joined APRP by June 2012. It was a good start, but the road wasn't easy.

I thought I'd be a shoe in for any APRP position. But, I think I was the only person who was interviewed three times for a post. My last interview was with FRI-C Director, two-star British Major General (MG) David Hook. He was concerned my background and connections in Afghanistan would make me a loose cannon operating outside FRI-C's bounds. The general reached out to the US Department of State and other places to find out more about me. Fortunately, the feedback was all positive. When I went to see him, he told me he already had my orders, so he wouldn't be able to turn me down even if he wanted to. My response was that it was important to make sure we all felt comfortable for me to be a team member. I reassured him I wasn't T. E. Lawrence ("Lawrence of Arabia"), despite my connections. MG Hook had also served in Kandahar, but our tours of duty didn't overlap.

I had already started FRI-C–related meetings. I went to see Masoom Stanakzai with Deputy Director Chris Landberg and Colonel Ginger Wallace (another AfPak Hand), who was in charge of FRI-C operations. I would not be in charge of anything, but would serve as a resource. Ginger was nice; I felt sure we'd work well together.

HPC offices were five minutes away by car from HQ ISAF. The compound was called Sedarat (the prime minister's office) because various prime ministers during the monarchy had had their offices there. At that time, the Afghan vice presidents' offices were located there, too. In the courtyard, roses were in full bloom. Stanakzai greeted us. I reminded him we'd met in Kandahar when he came with Rabbani for HPC's kickoff, but he didn't acknowledge meeting or remembering me—which I thought strange. I thought, maybe, like some, he'd size me up first before warming up. I supposed I was spoiled from having had such wonderful relationships (personal and professional) with folks at KPRT.

In the meantime, Captain Berg, Red Team director, kept reminding me that I was abandoning ship, using her naval metaphor. But she understood that I'd be more useful within an operational environment. Writing papers is not going to win the war, I told people!

Captain Berg asked me to accompany a few colleagues to Kabul City Hall to meet the Mayor on the twenty-eighth of May. Before we left, Deputy Director Nigel Little told me I'd have to translate. I replied I wasn't an interpreter and he should get one if he needed one. I informed him the only person I'd translated for, and only once, was Ambassador Karl Eikenberry who'd apologetically asked for help when he gave an interview to an Afghan reporter and wanted to be sure the message got through unchanged. That was in Arghandab, Kandahar, in October 2009. As it turned out, the late Mayor of Kabul spoke adequate English, and there was no need for an interpreter except when he didn't know the right words. He also had great difficulty understanding Little's Australian accent, especially when he mixed in broken Dari laced with an Australian twang.

Mayor Mohammad Younos Nawnadish, an ethnic Uzbek, greeted us in his huge office. I had been in his office thirty-nine years ago when an uncle was Mayor of Kabul in the early 1970s. He asked me who my uncle was; I told him Dost Mohammad Fazel, my mother's oldest brother. The Mayor said that he was a Russian-trained petroleum engineer. I told him that my uncle was a German-trained economist with an advanced degree from the University of Munich. He said, "Those were the days." (I was unsure whether he was being sarcastic, felt belittled, or what.) We moved on.

We discussed issues such as the city's unplanned expansion, population increase, and pollution. Nawnadish was determined to build more parks and make the mountains around Kabul green again. He had already planted over two million trees in Kabul, and he estimated the city's unabated growth to reach eight million people in the next five years.

He seemed very dynamic, but was a self-promoter. Everything revolved around him. He talked about his exploits in Europe and the United States and how he had impressed everyone by presenting himself as a modern man. At one conference in Baltimore, he related that participants were expecting a bearded mullah to introduce himself as Mayor of Kabul. "But, I totally surprised them with my slick suit and clean shaven face," he boasted.

That day, he was wearing a two-piece navy uniform (which looked like overalls) with a white shirt and necktie. I had to ask him whether he was making a fashion statement. He replied he often personally carried out inspections of roads and other projects and didn't want to ruin his suits. He also boasted about the appointment of two women in leadership positions at the municipality.

As we were leaving, he gave me two hefty books and one smaller one on the birth of Kabul, the major historical events of Kabul, and current happenings of the municipality. He accompanied us all the way to the front entrance of City Hall to bid us farewell.

On June 2, the Brits celebrated Queen Elizabeth II's Sixtieth Jubilee. The Canadians, Australians, and New Zealanders also participated. Although I didn't go, I could hear the sounds of marching bands from the garden.

I was anxiously awaiting flying home for R&R on June 4. I could hardly wait!

CHAPTER 8

7.22.2012
Gearing Up for HPC Activities

I returned to Kabul at the end of June after my R&R period at home. Although my trip was delayed twenty-four hours due to a flight cancellation, my return from leave was uneventful, but long and uncomfortable. I hoped that by then my accommodations would've improved, but to my chagrin, I returned to my old hole. On the bright side, a roommate had gone on R&R, which made the hole a little less crowded.

I started my new job at Force Reintegration Cell (FRI-C). I was a slow start, but I hoped that as time went by the pace would pick up. I went to the High Peace Council (HPC) and met with the chairman's political advisor, Amir Amin. He was about thirty-five, with a partial education in the United Kingdom. He came across as bright and forward looking and thinking, and he was very interested in my help.

The HPC, with seventy members from across the political, ethnic, tribal, and geographical spectrum and landscape of Afghanistan, set the tone for peace and reconciliation efforts. The Joint Secretariat (JS), although independent, was the executive-operational arm providing support for reintegration efforts throughout the country.

JS occupied a rickety building in Qala-e-Fatehullah Khan District. I tagged along with Colonel Ginger Wallace. I'd already met the person in charge, Minister Masoom Stanakzai. Although the politically charged reconciliation process hadn't gotten off to a good start, it was encouraging to see progress. Reintegration was aimed at foot soldiers and field commanders tired of fighting. By July, over five thousand people (up from over four thousand in June) had laid down arms to rejoin their communities.

These people had to renounce all violence, accept the Afghan constitution, submit to biometric procedures, and pass their local and national vetting processes, among other things. The program gave them a temporary six-month $120 monthly stipend to get back on their feet. A small grant program for community projects also helped sustain the village toward recovery and resiliency. Unsurprisingly, the number of those reintegrating was higher in the north and west than in the south, where security was worst.

But a fundamental problem was that HPC didn't work well with JS. There were many reasons for this disconnect, the chief problem being the personal relationship between the new HPC chair and the JS chief, Stanakzai. After Rabbani, the first HPC chair, was assassinated, Karzai appointed Rabbani's son to the position. The Rabbanis are ethnic Tajik from the north, belonging to the Jamiat Islami group. Stanakzai is Pashtun from Logar Province with a different political affiliation. Even though Stanakzai himself was wounded during Rabbani's assassination, he was accused by Rabbani's people of complicity in the killing.

Imagine how complicated and challenging it is to foster unity in Afghanistan! It is beyond exasperating—that's been inherent for centuries—although it can be done, given the right leadership, such as during King Zahir Shah's astute reign.

On Friday, July 6, I invited Anwar Hamidi to brunch at the Serena Hotel. Anwar is the brother of the late Mayor Hamidi of Kandahar, with whom I'd worked very closely and who was murdered the year before. Anwar was President Karzai's chief of protocol.

Serena is a hotel chain with locations mostly in Africa and owned by the Agha Khan family. It was the best hotel in Kabul, a world class facility. Serena was attacked a few years ago by insurgents and several people were killed. It seemed very secure in July 2012. Brunch was truly wonderful, consisting of all sorts of international and local fare. We sat at a table overlooking the beautiful rose garden, forgetting for a while that we were in Afghanistan.

We had a great time reminiscing about Mayor Hamidi and his sometimes crazy exploits. Anwar also mentioned that one of my cousins who lived in Rome was in town; he'd seen him a few days earlier at the funeral of one of King Zahir Shah's cousins. I told Anwar I'd like to see him.

That afternoon, my cousin Tariq called. Anwar had seen the Foreign Minister in the afternoon, who told him Tariq was around and had given him my cell phone number. I called Anwar to see if he could send his driver over to take me to the Afghan foreign minister's house to visit my cousin. But he'd already let the driver go since it was Friday, the day of rest for Afghans. The next day, Anwar sent his driver to take me to Foreign Minister Zalmai Rasool's home.

While Rasool was not the dynamic, competent person for this position that Afghanistan desperately needed, he had a medical degree from France and spoke three languages. After going through a dozen checkpoints and gates, I arrived at 11:00 a.m. As the crow flies it was only a mile from HQ ISAF. The last time I had seen my cousin was in Rome in 2010.

The week before, the Red Team's captain Colonel Heidi Berg asked me to accompany a couple of Red Teamers to meet the Governor of Parwan Province. Parwan is next to Kabul; its capital Charikar is sixty miles north of Kabul. I had to ask MG Hook for permission and he readily agreed. Sixty miles isn't that far, even in Afghanistan; we could've gone by ground convoy in the morning and returned in the afternoon. But, that would have been too logical and simple. Instead, we left on Sunday at 8:45 a.m. to go to Kabul Airport, where we waited a couple of hours. We boarded a puddle-jumper for the ten-minute flight to Bagram Air Field (BAF). BAF is another huge, sprawling base akin to Kandahar Air Field (KAF). There are about twenty to thirty thousand people who live and work at BAF.

We were met there by a sergeant driving a huge SUV and went to the billeting office to get the night's accommodations. Our party consisted of an Aussie, Nigel Little; a Canadian, Paul Dickson; an American colonel, Ted Lockhart; and myself. Confusion was rampant about the foreigners' ranks, which the billeting office decided weren't high enough for them to stay in the building. They were assigned a transient tent. But Colonel Lockhart argued forcibly, so they were given a room in the same building Ted and I were in.

In the afternoon, we strolled over to the PX. While checking things out, I heard a female voice cry out, "Uncle Abdul!" I turned and saw my niece Zohra, who lived in northern California. I couldn't believe it. What were the chances of an encounter such as this? She'd been at BAF for four months working as an interpreter. Seeing my cousin Tariq and my niece all in the short span of a week made for a very small world indeed!

We got up early on Monday, July 9 for our trip to the governor's office. We boarded four MRAP vehicles with three armed soldiers in each vehicle. After an hour, we arrived at 8:30 a.m. We parked the vehicles across the street in another facility and walked outside to get to the governor's compound.

We came upon a damaged building. Someone explained that insurgents had been able to breach security with the aim of killing the governor. The building had sustained major damage during the firefight. We went to the new building, past a huge conference room, and to the governor's equally enormous office. A big-screen TV was blaring away. A closed-circuit TV system showed all paths leading to his office. Not trusting anyone, he was evidently in charge of his own security.

The governor wasn't there, so we had lots of time to check out his office. The first item that caught my attention was a collection of photos on a tall credenza behind his desk. I recognized a few faces and names of previous governors, starting with those who had served King Zahir Shah. I pointed out that the picture arrangement spoke volumes about Afghanistan and what was presently wrong with it.

My group didn't get it, so I tried to explain. Governors who served the King were all educated: one had a PhD from Germany, while others were educated in the United States. The quality of personnel depicted in those photographs went down, moving from right to left, commensurate with various regimes after the monarchy was overthrown. They still didn't get it. Colonel Ted said, "Well, one can learn on the job." I asked him whether he'd be where he was without college and special training. I think he finally got the picture.

The governor finally arrived at 10:00 a.m. Abdul Basir Salangi is a three-star general in the Afghan National Police force, a monumental achievement for a person with only a grade school education. He was Kabul's Chief of Police before being appointed Governor of Parwan by Karzai. He belonged to the Northern Alliance group, thus taking his orders from First Vice President Marshal Fahim (another grade-school-educated man) and Bismillah Khan, the Interior Minister. They'd fought alongside Ahmad Shah Masood against other mujahedeen groups in the early 1990s and against the Taliban later. Salangi, now forty-eight, said he had taken up arms at seventeen. Karzai appointed him governor in a quid pro quo arrangement with Fahim—thereby keeping alive the system of patronage.

Salangi's favorite word was "kill," which he used numerous times during our meeting. In response to the ideas of peace and reconciliation he said, "No, but hell no." He reflected the attitude of Northern Alliance warlords who saw Taliban participation as against their interests; the only way to deal with them was to marginalize them. Salangi said his province was the most important in all of Afghanistan and that the United States should maintain a base there forever!

We had a helicopter flight back scheduled that afternoon, but it was commandeered by General Allen, the four-star in charge of it all. We waited until 8:30 p.m. for another chopper to Kabul, which took about twenty minutes. It was too late to make the four-mile trip to headquarters, so we spent the night on bare beds in a tent at IJC headquarters at KAIA.

The next morning, we were picked up by two armored SUVs. I got into the first vehicle. The morning traffic had started to gain momentum, and our drivers were maneuvering in and out of traffic to prevent any stoppage on the road due to security concerns. As we drove on a divided road in Wazir Akbar Khan, a woman appeared from out of nowhere to cross the street in front of us. We shouted, "Watch out! Watch out!" And although the young American soldier-driver tried to take evasive action, it was too late. The woman hit the ground. We stopped and a mob started gathering—which wasn't a good sign. Police officers dispersed the mob and had us pull over.

I was the only one who could speak Dari. Although I didn't get out of the vehicle when the mob was gathering, I got out later. We had to wait for the Traffic Investigation Unit to arrive. The victim, meanwhile, was thrown into a car and taken to the hospital. A young man said she was a cleaning lady at the Australian embassy. The traffic investigating officer finally showed up. He asked our American driver whether he owned a house, his salary, the names of his father, grandfather, cousins, uncles, nephews, and on and on, where he lived, how old he was, and on and on. Exhausting!

The accident happened at 7:05 a.m. By the time the investigator finished, it was 8:50 a.m. The usual procedure was to give them a form with our information and leave, but for some unknown reason the sergeant in charge of the convoy didn't do that. There were lots of people who wanted to harm us—two ISAF vehicles full of officers and civilians pinned down in one place for two hours was indeed dangerous. Luckily, nothing happened to us, and we were finally allowed to continue on. After another few minutes we found ourselves back in ISAF's secure compound. We later learned the woman's injuries were not too serious.

On July 14, we attended a peace and reconciliation event in Kandahar. We left at 5:00 a.m. for the airport. The Embassy Air plane, a Beach 1900D, took off at 7:45 a.m. for the one-and-a-half-hour flight to KAF, where we then boarded one of two Chinook helicopters with whirling rotors. The first stop was Camp Nathan Smith. Afghan officials in Kandahar were waiting, but I didn't see the governor among them, which was disappointing. We then took off for Zhari district.

Twenty minutes later, we landed amid a huge dust storm created by whirling helicopter rotors. It was a ten minute ride to Nalgham village, my first time there. Until recently, it was Taliban country. The convoy snaked through vineyards, lush orchards, and farmhouses made of mud. It was a hot day with a searing temperature of 111 degrees Fahrenheit.

The event kicked off on time with a recitation from the Quran followed by speeches, one echoing the other about the importance of peace and reconciliation. I was happy to see Kandahari dignitaries I had met before, and they were happy to see me, too. Some thought I'd returned, expressing disappointment when they heard my duty station was in Kabul.

Lunch was served on trays. It was platters of rice, lamb, chicken, and fruit for dessert. Three to four people shared a tray, with people eating from the same platter with their hands. We had disinfectant fluid with us which didn't wash off all the dirt. Oh well! It was 1:30 p.m. and time to leave. We'd removed our body armor, which unfortunately had been soaking up heat for several hours. For the next two hours, steel plates inside the armor gave off searing heat, like a sauna wrapped around the torso. I don't think I've been so hot, ever. The helicopters reversed course back to Kabul.

Even with the governor and High Peace Council chair absent, the meeting had turned out well. It was great to see Nalgham no longer in the hands of the Taliban; I hoped it would continue so. Many people told me that despite some spectacular attacks, the Taliban were on the defensive. They said signing the Afghan Strategic Agreement with the United States, for Afghanistan to be a major non-NATO ally of America, had made people hopeful. Property values in Kandahar had increased, another indication of people being hopeful.

I met Salahudin Rabbani, HPC chairman, in his private residence on July 16. I had met his father, Burhanudin Rabbani, in December 2010 in Kandahar when he kicked off the Afghan Peace and Reconciliation Program. I spent an hour with Salahudin Rabbani in the very same room his father was assassinated in. Salahudin told me he was looking forward to working with me. I would be spending at least three days a week at HPC working with a variety of staff members on urgent issues.

CHAPTER 9

8.14.2012:
Promoting Diplomacy in Advancing HPC's Goal for Reconciliation

The pace of life slowed down considerably in Afghanistan in late July and early August. This was the holy month of Ramadan, during which Muslims refrain from eating, drinking, smoking, sex, and other human desires from before dawn to dusk. Ramzan or Ramadan is the ninth month of the Islamic calendar, when the Quran was revealed to Prophet Mohammad. Based on lunar movement, it advances ten days each year relative to solar-based calendars because the lunar year is shorter. For the next few years, Ramadan would occur during the longest and hottest days, making it even more difficult to endure.

Ramadan is a spiritual time to cleanse body and soul, reflect on life, and understand what the less fortunate go through by experiencing hunger, thirst, and other forms of deprivation. But children, pregnant or nursing women, the sick, and the elderly are not required to fast. People such as doctors, pilots, leaders, and others whose judgments and actions could possibly inflict adverse consequences on others if they were impaired by fasting are also exempt. Those who cannot fast, should not fast, and those who have the means are required to feed the poor for a month.

But, very few people follow these rules. I found out President Karzai fasted. But he was diabetic with huge responsibilities relative to people's lives and well-being, so according to dogma, he shouldn't have been fasting to ensure he made sane decisions.

Ramadan is also a time to reflect on the positive qualities of kindness, forgiveness, peace, and unconditional love. People are to use their limbic brain more than their reptilian one to stay away from anger, aggression, and killing. In short, if people adhered to the letter and spirit of Ramadan, everything would be hunky-dory. Unfortunately, killing, aggression, and mean-spiritedness continue to firmly grip this Muslim nation.

While there's been a huge problem with Abrahamic religions (Judaism, Christianity, and Islam) throughout history, other religions are not immune to such tendencies either. Human beings have a tendency to pervert religion for personal and/or political gains. We've seen violence by certain adherents of Hinduism, Buddhism, Sikhism, and other sects. Ideologies such as communism and Nazism, while purporting to transform society for the better, have also carried out unimaginable atrocities in the name of political expediencies.

During Ramadan, people fuel up on food and drink at 3:00 a.m. for the next sixteen hours of abstinence. Official work hours are from 7:00 a.m. to 1:00 p.m., but most people don't show up until 9:00 a.m. or 10:00 a.m., only to leave around noon. In some Arab countries, people party all night long until just before dawn and sleep all day, which may be a way of coping with Ramadan's hardships, but completely misses the point!

Trying to get things done in Afghanistan is a challenge under the best of circumstances. But, shorter working hours, combined with hunger-thirst deprivation and short-tempered functionaries, it becomes a real problem to operate a functional society.

This caused another problem where we lived. Cleaners arrived at 7:00 a.m. to clean our bathrooms instead of later in the day. This was the time I'd come back from the gym to shave and shower, like others on my floor. Getting cleaned up with two janitors washing and wiping around you was not the most pleasant morning experience.

The international community in Afghanistan (ISAF and embassies) prevailed upon the spirit of Ramadan for cordial outreach by inviting Afghan officials to "Iftar" dinners. An Iftar dinner breaks fasting, after dusk. My boss, MG Hook, invited four people from the HPC for Iftar. HPC being my bailiwick, I got to send out invitations.

A "safe house" just outside HQ ISAF enabled us to meet and entertain Afghans who preferred not to come to HQ. This two-story villa in the

Green Zone was a five-minute walk from ISAF's main gate. It had a nice lawn, rose bushes, trees, and even a few grape vines.

The military plans everything to the extreme. For this Iftar dinner, an American major and a lieutenant colonel were in charge. They started two weeks prior and met daily to make sure things were on track. I couldn't take it anymore. I finally said, "Folks, relax, this is just a dinner. People arrive, sit down, eat dinner, talk, and say good bye. That's it!" This is a small, but good, example of why military operations are so costly. The dinner happened exactly as I'd predicted. What a genius I am.

Guest Abdul Hakim Mojahid was a former Talib who came to the United States to represent the Taliban in the late 1990s. He was HPC's first vice chair. Second Vice Chair Ludin was a no show. Maulana Waqad, outreach committee chair, brought his son. The other guest was HPC chair advisor, Amir Ramin. People in charge of the safe house had prepared quite a spread of turnovers, dumplings, dishes of rice, chicken, lamb, kebab, and dessert. We talked about many things, but the peace process, its myriad challenges and its future, dominated our conversations.

A week later, when ISAF Commander, General Allen, gave a small Iftar dinner, one of the servers was a US Army major! As expected, planning for this event was even more complicated and elaborate! Allen's guests were Chairman Rabbani, Joint Secretariat's Director Stanakzai, and Minister of Religious Affairs, Niazi. From our side, we were my boss MG Hook and me. Two Afghan American interpreters took turns with translations. The Religious Affairs Minister was the only one needing help, as Rabbani and Stanakzai were both fluent in English.

This Iftar conversation was much more interesting. General Allen talked about the importance of the role of religious scholars for the peace process. Rabbani talked about his recent trip to Saudi Arabia and the support he received there not only from the government, but also from religious leaders. Stanakzai said that he believed that after international forces leave, a reason for insurgents inciting people to fight would be eliminated—with mullahs calling upon people to lay down arms. He felt that scholars should work hard telling people not to fight their own people. Niazi, the Minister of Religious Affairs, didn't participate much.

After our guests left, General Allen reiterated, "The effort to bring peace to Afghanistan has the highest priority in this headquarters." Thus I felt that my efforts in working with the High Peace Council played an important role. MG Hook told General Allen about my background and why I was chosen for this slot. He replied, "Very good choice."

General Allen reminisced about the late Mayor Hamidi of Kandahar City whom I'd mentored during my State Department tour in Kandahar. He called Hamidi a very brave man, saying that his killing was very tragic for Afghanistan. I concurred. Although I'd met General Allen a couple of times before, this was the first time we'd engaged in conversation. But even prior to this interaction, I was very impressed with him. He's very nice to everyone, intelligent, and came across as genuine.

At the beginning of August, I participated in a three day Afghan Hands Conference. I was an Afghan Hand, but 99 percent of Afghan Hands were military officers, from colonel to captain, plus a few noncommissioned officers. Typically, about 160 Hands in Afghanistan worked closely with their Afghan counterparts throughout the country. Afghan Hands underwent extensive language and cultural training before deploying to Afghanistan. At least in theory, they could establish better working relationships with Afghans.

A speaker at the conference was General Allen. He talked for half an hour about the mission and the role of Hands. He was eloquent, lucid, and so relevant that he gave the impression of using an invisible teleprompter.

It was an interesting conference. Various Hands talked about their unique experiences from different parts of the country. We exchanged ideas, asked for help, and the whole nine yards. Many Hands were engaged in the Afghan Peace and Reintegration Program in the provinces. A number of us from my organization (F-RIC) gave presentations. I talked about HPC and challenges in engaging locals to do more for peace.

Three Important Points

1. <u>**Green-on-Blue**</u>

"Green-on-blue" refers to violence inflicted by Afghan security forces on international personnel. (The Afghan army uniform is greenish.) There were thirty-seven green-on-blue incidents in 2012, two more than the previous year. Although the Taliban always claimed responsibility for these acts, only a small number could be attributed to Taliban infiltrations. The majority were due to cultural insensitivities and mundane arguments escalating out of proportion. But the effects were unfortunately the same, in distancing the members of the international community from their Afghan counterparts.

Consequently, we were under strict orders to conform to security rules such as travelling to Afghan offices with an armed guardian angel. This phenomenon, the "collaborators' dilemma," has also been seen in other conflicts. People in the host nation who had previously collaborated feel abandoned and want to establish their independence and credibility in case the insurgents become victorious. This was the case in Afghanistan when we announced our withdrawal for 2014. Unfortunately, how we would leave was not fully explained to Afghans when the policy was announced—which caused lots of uneasy feelings.

When the US government signed the Afghan Strategic Partnership Agreement and made Afghanistan a notable non-NATO ally people became more hopeful they wouldn't be abandoned. The Tokyo Conference in July 2012 also improved the mood. In Tokyo, the international community announced continuing economic and political support for Afghanistan. These events produced tangible, albeit unnoticed, results. In reflecting this confidence, property values in Kabul and some provinces such as Kandahar increased.

2. <u>**Afghan Security Forces Casualties**</u>

Every day some of us participated in the ISAF commander's standup meeting either in person or, more often, via closed-circuit TV or intranet. The briefing lasted an hour, during which the commander was briefed about anything and everything that had happened in the last twenty-four hours.

A briefer presented slides of casualties from both Afghans and the coalition. General Allen took a keen interest in these slides and asked many questions.

It was obvious the number of Afghan casualties was rising. Many were reported killed and wounded every day. Why? Because mostly Afghans were in the forefront of fighting by that time; they were leading more operations, and more of them were in the field. Training, too, was cause for concern, as was their cavalier attitude of not wearing helmets and body armor. Although it was sad that casualty numbers were higher, the good news was Afghans were doing the fighting and taking on more responsibility for their country's security.

3. Comparisons with the Soviets Experience

To my and other people's dismay, it became fashionable to draw parallels between our mission and the Soviets' misadventures in Afghanistan. These people clearly showed their lack of understanding of two very different situations. During the Afghan Hands conference, I set one person straight. While there were some tactical similarities between the international mission in Afghanistan and the Soviets' foray lasting ten years, there were no parallels.

For starters, the Soviets took a stable country and spurred negative forces into breaking it apart. By contrast, the international community was trying to put this society together again—after chasing out Al-Qaeda from Afghanistan.

Afghans knew this very well. Although people supporting our efforts declined from over 95 percent in 2002 to about 50 percent a decade later, the Soviets were universally hated in 2012. The Soviets drew support from puppet communists who probably consisted of less than 1 percent of the population. Many other reasons prevail, which would require writing a book to examine and explain very complicated scenarios.

CHAPTER 10

8.21.2012:
Afghans Celebrate Holidays with Gusto!

When Ramadan finally came to an end, there was much speculation whether it would end on August 18 or 19. Why? It always depends on sighting the moon to determine the end of one month and the beginning of the next. After a month-long fasting, the three-day celebration of "Eid-el-Fitr" gives people an opportunity to don new (or best) clothes, visit family and friends, drink tea, eat sweets, and enjoy each other's company. Parents and close relatives or elders give money to kids, called "Eidie."

After the pace of life slowed down during Ramadan, that year, the three-day holiday, weekends, and Afghan Independence Day conspired to make a full week of leave-taking. It was welcome relief for us as well, to catch up on paperwork and kick back a bit.

My routine was to get up at 5:30 or 6:00 a.m., hit the gym for an hour, Skype Catherine, have breakfast, and be off to the office between 7:30 and 8:30 a.m. I crashed around 9:30 p.m., sometimes later. On Sundays we typically started at 10:00 a.m., on Fridays at noon, pretty much a seven day work week. I still share a room with two others, making quiet time and privacy a luxury I desperately desire, not to mention the lost luxury of getting a good night's sleep.

Yikes, it was easy to lose one's sanity in that "medium-security prison." Factor in work frustrations, delays, dealing with difficult people, security concerns, lousy food, ad nauseum—and the place became a dangerous funny farm, fast. I hoped to catch a few afternoon naps during the holidays!

August 16 was my last trip to HPC offices before breaking for Eid. I went with my guardian angel, along with David Warner, a British colonel, and his armed companion in a two-armored SUV convoy. HPC offices are in the vice president's compound just outside Green Zone, a five minute drive from HQ ISAF.

Our vehicles had special passes to enter the compound. Beautiful rose gardens and trees surrounded the driveway and parking lot. We took a left turn to a marble building and got dropped off at the entrance. The compound had many other office buildings.

The marble building towering high above the others was built in the last five years. National Directorate for Security (NDS) guards manned the entrance just inside building's main foyer. NDS was like the FBI, CIA and Secret Service all rolled into one. It was also responsible for the security of some government facilities. Most NDS employees were former agents of an organization called Khidmate Ettelat-e Dawlati (State Intelligence Services) organized by the KGB in the 1980s. NDS guards were mostly illiterate, low-level personnel. The entrance had a metal detector with an X-ray machine. There was always a problem getting in with guns (which were concealed). Some days we walked right in, while on others we had to go back and forth for ten minutes.

That morning my partner and I had no problem. But, they wouldn't let in Colonel Warner and his buddy, who were both armed. After intense negotiations we struck a compromise allowing one person to carry arms into the building. During the commotion, a guard asked the colonel (who was in civilian clothes) his rank. To which he replied, "Colonel in the British army." The sandal-wearing, disheveled guard said he was a colonel, too. I could hardly contain myself and let out an audible sound of disbelief!

I said under my breath, I remember what colonels were like when the going was good, mister; you're not one of them, not even remotely close. This may sound elitist, but I often wished not to have lived during the country's better times. It would have been easier for me to accept the current situation and move on. But, every day, I was painfully reminded of how far Afghanistan had descended into the abyss.

After clearing the guard hurdle, we had two choices to ascend to the fourth floor. The first was to take the elevator, which many opt for. But I discouraged people from it because power was not reliable. I didn't want to get stuck in any elevator, let alone in Afghanistan. The second choice was obviously taking the stairs—more beneficial for our health as well.

The first order of business that day was for HPC Chair Salahudin Rabbani to record TV and radio spots with a "wish you well" message for Eid and to convey the message of peace, reconciliation, and unity. I complimented him on both message and delivery. His next meeting was with our chief of development and finance, Mark Revell, a Brit who had started a month ago.

The purpose of that meeting was to explain the budgeting process, expenditures to date, projects, and other matters. The meeting went well, except that my guardian angel, a US Navy lieutenant commander (also an Afghan Hand), would cut people off and interject his opinions. This was not good, although Rabbani would nod politely. Unfortunately, there were people who didn't know much about protocol and wanted to make their presence known—regardless of circumstances. It was my job as the chairman's handler to exercise damage control, so I'd gently say, "Good point, but we'll have to discuss it another time."

Rabbani asked me to stay after our meetings. He wanted to know how my engagements with HPC members had been going, and what they thought about him. I explained by borrowing from "The Good, The Bad, and The Ugly" (the title of one of my favorite spaghetti westerns growing up in Kabul). I told him I'd come across the good (willing to work), the bad (skeptics), and the ugly (unbelievers in the peace process). My advice was to promote the good, reach out to the bad and try to change their minds, but not to waste time on the ugly.

I told him his good ideas needed to be shared to establish his credibility. He liked the advice and promised to increase his outreach to the bad and do more to empower the good. Rabbani is a Tajik from the north; the Pashtuns viewed Tajiks suspiciously given the murky atmosphere of ethnic distrust and political competition. He said he also planned to visit Pashtun's southern and eastern provinces to talk to people there directly.

The message Rabbani taped was only the first step in a more comprehensive strategic communication ("stratcomm" in military lingo) we were working on with Afghans. The first anniversary of Rabbani's father's death would fall on September 20 that year. To commemorate his death, HPC and the Afghan government were organizing a Week of Peace and Unity with our help, consisting of TV and radio messages paid for by us, a religious conference on peace with participants from other Islamic countries, a meeting of provincial governors on peace and reintegration, and other events—culminating in a gathering of notables and an address by President Karzai.

August 19 is Independence Day. We received an e-mail about fireworks scheduled for the night, and therefore, they were no cause for alarm. What a contrast to Afghanistan's Independence Day celebrations in the past!! At 8:00 p.m., I stepped outside and saw a few bursts of paltry fireworks high above the city.

At the conclusion of the third Anglo-Afghan War on 8 August, 1919, the British government declared Afghanistan a sovereign nation. The war began on 8 May, 1919 when the Afghan army invaded British India. It ended on 8 August with an armistice followed by the Rawalpindi conference which recognized Afghanistan's full independence. It also formalized the Durand line as the de facto boundary between Afghanistan and British India. The first British military foray began in 1839, only to end in disaster in January 1842. A Doctor Brydon and fifty others who surrendered were the only survivors out of a force of sixteen thousand five hundred military and civilian combatants. The British sent in another expeditionary force in 1878 to avenge the massacre of the first war, also known as the Second Anglo-Afghan war, which lasted till 1880.

Back in the days of my youth in Afghanistan, Independence Day celebrations ("Jashin") lasted seven days, typically starting a couple of weeks after the eighteenth so the weather would be cooler. Schools were out for at least three days. Celebrations kicked off on the first morning with a military parade past the royal stand for King Zahir Shah to review. Another parade in the afternoon proudly showed off Boy and Girl Scout troops, university students, athletes, and other professional groups at the stadium where the King, Queen, and Crown Prince watched from the royal box. (In contrast, the Taliban had used this very stadium during their rule for public executions.)

People descended on Kabul from other provinces. Buzkashi games were held. The real parties took place at night. Many of Kabul's streets and boulevards were decorated with lights. In Chaman-e-Hozoori (His Majesty's Lawn), all the Afghan ministries and government agencies pitched tents (some had permanent structures) for musicians and performers, and restaurants served food. It was a total celebration of Independence in every sense of the word. Jashin was by far the most important and biggest event in the country, including religious ones!

In 2012, a new crescent moon was sighted on August 19, thereby ushering in a new Islamic month and year with Eid-el-Fitr.

My workload had diminished, but I had nowhere to go to rest up. I was able to take a forty minute nap one day, a needed and welcome relief. The rat race would starts anew on the twenty-third. However, I made reservations to return home on October 12. Although it was a while off, I was counting the days. I had no plans to travel once I got home for the two and a half weeks of R&R.

For an explanation of Buzkashi see www.afghan-network.net/Culture/buzkashi.html.

CHAPTER 11

9.4.2012:
Modifying Perceptions for Afghanistan's Peaceful Socioeconomic Transition

Because of the disturbing trend of comparing the Soviet experience in Afghanistan with our involvement—it was sometimes presented as a strategy in our moving forward—I'd like to offer some reflections and analyses.

On August 22, I was invited to a meeting where a Department of Defense human terrain specialist gave a presentation on this very subject. The presenter was a short, stocky guy trying to hide his belly under a shirt. He hadn't showered for a while, given his offensive body odor. I didn't pay much attention to his name until he started talking in heavily accented Russian English.

"Let me tell you about myself. My name is Timothy Gusinov. I am a social scientist with the Special Forces Human Terrain. I was a Soviet officer with extensive combat experience in Afghanistan in the 1980s," he said. I cringed when I heard he had combat experience. "I immigrated to the United States in 1993," he continued. I almost interrupted him to ask, "How many Afghans did you kill during your combat days here?" The Soviets were responsible for the deaths of at least a million Afghans. The international community today is still paying to clear land mines. Two decades after the Soviet defeat and withdrawal from Afghanistan, these mines continue to maim and kill Afghan children!

I itched to destroy Gusinov's false entreaties, but didn't want to hog the stage. However, I left no doubt in everyone's minds about where I stood. I told them that being subjected to such one-sided information without the proper context isn't helpful. MG Hook agreed that without the proper political context, the presentation was skewed.

We really need to clarify and weed out misunderstandings at every opportunity! Only then can we hope to engage in modifying perceptions—to gradually reap behavioral buy-in to regain support for our mission here and abroad.

With the situation deteriorating with resurgent insurgencies in the previous five years, doubters in Washington and elsewhere who were resigned to the notion that we were getting out of Afghanistan without accomplishing our mission saw this involvement as a failure—and failures must be explained away.

However, I believe that while there were some technical and tactical similarities, there were NO overarching parallels between our and Russian engagements in Afghanistan.

How do we explain "the failure"? It is an excuse to say that the Soviets failed, despite many advantages, and it is therefore unrealistic for us to fare any better.

The Red Army enjoyed the advantages of a long common border, a closed society with no citizen accountability, highly centralized decision-making in Moscow with no checks and balances, and a vast conscript army from regional republics, some of whom shared a common language with Afghans.

Looking at these two situations superficially would lead anyone to believe they are similar. But they just aren't. Two examples illustrate my point.

First, the Soviets took over a country, initially by proxy and later directly, which was a viable nation state. In 1978, communists took over Afghanistan with a bloody coup. Less than two years later, these communists were on the verge of collapse, and it was opportune for the Soviets to invade Afghanistan with 150,000 troops to prop up the regime they'd installed. The Soviets had smartly and quietly set in motion forces that broke Afghanistan apart with devastating consequences: for Afghans, and later for the United States, the region, and the international community. We came in to help Afghans pick up the pieces—after twenty years of strife and warfare initiated by the Soviets.

Finding and putting back broken pieces of a society wreaked by such havoc and devastation, and for such a long time, isn't easy. What makes it even more difficult is that the longer a society's in turmoil, the more complex societal problems (ethnic and tribal divisions) become. They spawn a multi-generational specter for locals to eliminate, while facing a tremendous lack of resources from the human to the financial.

Another major difference is that the Soviets were universally hated. The depth of their support was less than 1 percent of Afghans, limited to communists who numbered a few thousand at best. When we (the United States and the international community) came to Afghanistan in 2001, over 95 percent of Afghans supported ISAF. Even with this support dwindling due to mistakes we made and other reasons, about half of Afghans continued supporting our mission and didn't want us to leave.

Eid came and ended on August 21, but Afghans continued their break as President Karzai declared Wednesday, August 22 a holiday. Thursday was a "bridge day," with Friday being the official day of rest, thus making this one of the longest Eids in history.

On August 26, we were to go to Logar Province, southeast of Kabul. The night before, after I was in bed, my cell phone rang. It was General Ghareeb, HPC's Provincial Affairs Liaison. He said the governor of Logar was in Kabul with his aide and needed to go along with us. We were to meet at 6:30 a.m. Changing the flight manifest was not easy at the last minute, not to mention that I was no trip coordinator. I got dressed and went to the office and was pleasantly surprised to see Jon Sowers, the navy commander arranging the trip, still there. He said we might be able to get the governor on board with us, but possibly not his aide.

At 6:30 a.m., a group of Afghans waited outside ISAF gate. Three HPC members who were supposed to be going with us didn't turn up. Their job was to bring peace to the country, but they didn't bother. However, this meant that the governor's aide could now be accommodated. We drove to a nearby base, North Kabul Compound to take a helicopter out to Logar and land fifteen minutes later. Czech Republic soldiers escorted us to the provincial governor's building. About fifty people were in the conference room. We took our seats; nothing happened. Then suddenly, there was a flurry of activity—people rushed in to spread out a repast of bread, tea, milk, yogurt, jam, and lamb kebabs. It was time for breakfast.

After breakfast, the governor opened the meeting by blaming every ill on Kabul, absolving himself of any responsibility. Then the mayhem began! Speaker after speaker pointed fingers at each other and complained bitterly about Logar Provincial Peace Council's inability to address grievances or cajole insurgents to lay down arms to rejoin their communities. Both the council chair and the deputy resigned on the spot. More uncertainty ensued; the meeting broke up into smaller groups. We ate lunch and resumed.

Nafisa dominated the conversation nonstop for a good half hour. Afghan women are usually reserved, but not Nafisa. She talked about her childhood, children, love, and discoursed on the virtue of cleanliness, admonishing the men to wash more often. "I never leave the house before washing myself," she urged. I whispered to a colleague I feared for her life. Lo and behold, she proclaimed: "I'm at peace with myself. If they (Taliban, mujahedeen) kill me, I forgive them!"

The governor announced the general consensus on a new chair and a new deputy as HPC representatives. The gentlemen were introduced, with a couple of brief speeches thrown in; the disgruntled were satisfied, and they sang kumbaya. Voila, democracy Afghan style! Lots can be said about Afghanistan's traditional consensus-making (and peace-keeping) processes. We could learn a lot and adapt it to our needs.

We returned to Kabul without the governor, but with the rest of the Afghan delegation from HPC's Joint Secretariat. Wowza! We were once again instrumental in connecting Afghans with Afghans. Whether it was for real and how long it would last, was up to them.

I received an interesting article Dan Bumstead, the fearless leader of our "Great Decisions" group, had kindly sent me. "Great Decisions" is a series of eight annual discussions organized by Naples Council on World Affairs. Topics are chosen by the Foreign Policy Association, written up by subject matter experts, and published in the Foreign Policy Association handbook. The program begins in late January and goes eight weeks. Our group (one of the largest) meets once weekly on Tuesdays. A member assigned a topic gives a ten-minute presentation (sometimes more, depending on the reliability of the timer manned by our leader). That's followed by wine, cheese, crackers, assorted snacks, and a great discussion. Food for mind and body.

The article, NATO, Post-2014 Afghanistan, and the Energy Dimensions of Security, *published by the Institute for the Analysis of Global Security, projected the political and power structure after draw down. On this, I must say it was anyone's guess, but I went along with the idea that the central Afghan government in Kabul would control the larger cities.*

However, I believed that the rest of the country would be ruled by Taliban and warlords as the article also foresees. In my opinion, it would become area-dependent. For example, the south and parts of the Pashtun belt in the east would be Taliban country, while the north would be controlled by Northern Alliance warlords, who were already de facto rulers of these provinces.

As the article rightly stipulated, the economic growth of any country depends on the availability of cheap energy. That's the case in a functional system already working with national cohesion, some economic foundation, capacity, security, and other basic necessities—which, unfortunately, Afghanistan lacks (regardless of considerable progress in the ten years after the country was headed under the Taliban).

It'd be a mistake to talk about a national Afghan economy. Instead, we should look at the Kabul economy, provincial economies, district economies, and perhaps economies by sectors such as agriculture and light industries. In other words, there were lots of disparities in Afghanistan and the economy was one on which we couldn't generalize.

In America, we've been through the dot com bubble and the housing bubble, among others. The Afghan economy was the biggest bubble of all—the war economy bubble. Translating this into comprehensible terms, it means that (1) a disproportionate few became überrich, (2) a few were doing okay working for us and other war-related activities, and (3) large swaths of the country were still living in abject poverty. Although the international community offered some guarantees to ensure Afghanistan wouldn't collapse after our draw down, the country would eventually have to undergo a huge correction. The Afghan bubble would inevitably burst like other bubbles—similar to the Hegelian concept of having to rebuild from the ashes.

Afghanistan could hopefully rekindle its economy with a more stable foundation based on a viable nation-state's basic amenities, which are listed above. Only then would the need arise to increase energy production to fuel a growing economy. Strategically, many countries were excited to extract Afghanistan's raw materials. In fact, the Chinese signed lucrative deals to their advantage with the Afghan government.

I finally got to drive for the first time on the streets of Kabul after thirty-six years—in an armored Toyota Land Cruiser. It wasn't comfortable handling such a top-heavy vehicle, and I had to drive aggressively too, in a very congested city wearing body armor and helmet. What possessed me? Dire necessity! I needed a driving certificate to self-drive in Kabul for more flexibility meeting Afghan officials. What a contrast to the good old days when I was in high school, cruising around town with my friends in my own car!

CHAPTER 12

9.18.2012:

Children Are Extinguished, Like Moths Drawn to a Deadly Flame

I was at my desk last Saturday, September 8, when suddenly, around 11:00 a.m., I was jolted by a loud blast. I jumped out of my chair and said, "That's not good." Sure enough, loud speakers blared out semicomprehensible sounds: "Lockdown, lockdown" and other warnings. It was an explosion outside HQ ISAF's gate, so powerful that debris cleared the compound's high blast walls to land in a parking lot inside.

The first thing that came to mind was the well-being of the little children who work as hawkers right outside the wire. Four of the dead included these kiddie peddlers. Photos of the little ones and their identities were published in the newspapers.

Among the dead were two sisters. Salma was thirteen and Parwana, eight. Kids typically hung out at the gate, running back and forth to foreigners at Camp Eggers in the Green Zone a few minutes away. Girls and boys (some carrying small backpacks) peddled gum, scarves, woven bracelets, and other cheap trinkets. I never bought anything from them, but occasionally gave them, including Parwana, a dollar bill.

Salma was in third grade, Parwana in second, they said. But I didn't believe them with their constant presence at the gate, which didn't leave time for school. I asked them where they lived; they said, "Shuhada-e-Saleheen." I know this area. It includes a huge cemetery where my father, grandparents, and other relatives are resting in peace, at least five miles from HQ ISAF. I couldn't imagine how these kids went back and forth, especially at night. (One said they went on foot, usually in groups.)

"Parwana" means butterfly, or a moth that adores a burning candle. This fatal attraction to flutter around a burning flame causes the moth to be finally consumed by it. Our sweet little butterfly fluttering around to attract a few dollars never realized the invisible cold spark of death would suddenly snatch away her life, too. Who'd think the Green Zone's security could be breached? Not these little ones, for sure! Sadly, this tragic event didn't persuade survivors to stop hawking there.

What were the alternatives? Parwana, her cohorts, and fellow fluttering moths shared one common anomaly—in being falsely attracted to an illusion that cost them their lives.

The news reported a fourteen-year-old boy was duped into carrying an explosive-laden backpack close to the gate for remote detonation. This boy didn't belong to Parwana's group. For, like typical gangs in inner city neighborhoods, resident hawkers sprang into action to defend their territories. They wouldn't allow strange kids to peddle in their territory, to cut into their profits. Additionally, this gang had to pay off Afghan police officers manning various checkpoints to peddle in the Green Zone. One day, I saw a little one run to a checkpoint to pay off the police. My heart just sank.

Little wonder then Parwana and her gang confronted the stranger who was only a few hundred feet shy of his intended destination—ISAF gate. During the ensuing scuffle his remote handler pressed the control button, detonating and lighting up the fatal "candle" consuming Parwana the butterfly, her older sister, and other kids.

One thing's for sure, unbeknown to them, Ms. Butterfly and her gang saved many lives—of people who didn't even realize it! We planned a memorial service and collected donations for the children's families.

As insurgents increased attacks, children's casualty rates went up, too. About 19 percent more kids lost their lives in 2012, compared to the previous year. Many were blown to pieces when vehicles hit Improvised Explosive Devices (IEDs) hidden along roads. The overwhelming majority of civilian casualties (CIVCAS in military lingo), over 80 percent, were caused by insurgents; less than 10 percent were caused by the coalition's collateral damage, including vehicular accidents.

The situation became tense at that time partly due to the upcoming 9/11 anniversary and a video release depicting Prophet Mohammad as a buffoon, womanizer, and pedophile. Afghans and Muslims don't understand our First Amendment governing the right to free speech. They think America's president, with a simple stroke of a pen, can change the law and stop the production of such lawless materials. They think stopping these incendiary productions would've saved the lives of Ambassador Christopher Stevens and others in Benghazi, Libya.

Westerners don't comprehend how people in traditional societies go crazy over a perceived blasphemous video or cartoon, leading to bloodshed—even though their religion condemns it. For, while many Muslims are terribly offended by any disrespect to Mohammad, Moses, Jesus, and other biblical prophets, they don't act up like crazy fringe extremists. People in Afghanistan take blasphemous disrespect very personally because they revere the Prophet as the most important member of their family.

It's very unfortunate that extremist groups dictate the general agenda. Too, since bad news sells, the media go berserk in whooping up and sensationalizing these incidents—further catalyzing and agitating negative consequences.

We were put under lockdown, unable to venture out to interact with Afghan officials. Working in a war situation and within that environment came with many inherent risks. I don't encourage a cavalier attitude. We should make every attempt to minimize dangers, but at the same time do our jobs well, or go on home.

But, as I've mentioned before, there were those who rarely left the compound. I didn't know what they contributed to our efforts—except to further their own careers and interests. I found out that two reservist lieutenant colonels with Red Team, my previous organization, received Bronze Stars at the end of their tours. They were never in combat and rarely ventured out, spending their entire time in the office writing papers.

On September 17, we organized an event for a HPC committee, including dinner, at HQ ISAF. A general would brief guests on the Afghan National Army's capabilities. The second part would entail taking VIPs to Camp Scorpion where they'd see a staged event by Afghan Special Operations Forces (SOF) raiding a village house.

Like everything military, the event was set in motion a month prior by issuing a Fragmentary Order. This is how orders are issued to accomplish most things in a war zone, from releasing prisoners to organizing special events. The planning begins with the first stage in identifying guests, then generating invitations, assigning seats, organizing interpreters, ordering food, and so on and so on; quite exhausting. On event day, everyone hopes for guests to arrive on time, and everyone's ready when the helicopters arrive after dinner to take them to post-dinner events.

We invited eleven people, including the HPC chair and two women on the executive committee. The day before, the chair and spokesman, Maulawi Kashaf, announced he couldn't make it. Two hours before the event, both women sent word that they couldn't come; one had food poisoning, while the other's kid was ill. The highest ranking official after the chair, Abdul Hakim Mujahid, former Taliban ambassador to the United Nations, was a half hour late. Some guests wanted to bring their vehicles in; some guests could be walked in through the gate. I waited outside for the last guest who wanted to bring in his vehicle. He was greeted by ISAF Deputy Commander LTG Bradshaw, a three-star British general.

Somehow, regardless of sterling efforts, the plan went wrong. When I entered the conference room with the last guest, I couldn't find my name card at the table. This meant I'd to sit in a chair behind the guests. But, this was a no-no because I work with these people on regularly; if they so much as caught a faint whiff I was not that important in the pecking order, my credibility would be undermined and I wouldn't be effective working with them. I pulled up a chair to the table, even though there was no place setting for me to eat dinner. But that was okay.

Guests ate hurriedly while listening to the PowerPoint presentation on the Afghan National Army's capabilities. They left for evening prayers, and then were escorted to the adjacent soccer field with waiting Black Hawks, rotors whirling and generating gusts of wind.

There was a slight glitch, but we finally boarded the birds. Once airborne, it took a few minutes to land at Camp Scorpion. We were bussed to the range, a short distance off. An SOF colonel briefed the VIPs on what to expect, eloquently parrying a legal question on the constitutionality of raiding people's homes.

We were handed night vision goggles, and the game was on! The Afghan SOFs looked exactly like their American counterparts with the same arms and equipment. Everyone was impressed with the show, which was followed by firing of live rounds. At the end, the Afghan Ministry of Defense's Chief of Staff, Karimi, a four-star general partially educated in the United States, told dignitaries they'd only seen the tip of the iceberg. He hoped to invite them back later for more.

This was a very busy week with an international conference on peace and other events including trips to other provinces. But I was getting closer to R&R, only three weeks away!

CHAPTER 13

10.1.2012:
High Peace Council Takes the High Road to Peace

The Afghan Week of National Peace and Unity coincided with the first anniversary of the death of the former HPC chair, Burhanudin Rabbani.

The week's events included TV and radio spots in local languages (Dari and Pashto) to spread the message of peace. The younger Rabbani was very articulate in his on-air spots. Another TV clip highlighted Parwana's mother and sisters on their loss.

In the clip, Parwana's mother stated that she was devastated to see her two girls come home in coffins that fateful day. They were not girls: "I considered them my boys as they helped provide for their family," she said. (While this may sound strange, a traditional society like Afghanistan's has more possibilities for males than females. It's a culturally correct compliment to refer to these girls as boys—given their effectiveness, bravery, and capabilities.) A little sister lamented no one would help with homework. The mother begged for peace, saying that enough was enough; her girls were gone. People needed to stop this carnage!

I accompanied HPC's First Vice President Mujahid and Rohani, another HPC member, to Khost Province in eastern Afghanistan along the Pakistani border. Both men were former Taliban. Khost is a restive province. It was my first return after forty-five years. As kids, my sister Zarmina and I visited when our father was the area's brigade commander. Then, it was part of Paktiya Province, but it had become a proper province run by its own governor. Khost is a vibrant city, with a university built by the United Arab Emirates.

RETURN TO KABUL

We boarded an Embassy Air MI8 Russian helicopter around 8:00 a.m. at a corner of Kabul Airport specially reserved for Embassy Air. We landed fifty minutes later at Camp Salerno. From the helipad, we were driven to the main gate where we were supposed to be met by the governor. But there was no sign of him, and we were told to wait for vehicles to drive us into town for the event.

This event was scheduled around a ribbon-cutting ceremony for a new building for peace and reintegration activities. One Afghan National Police (ANP) truck was allowed to enter the base. Two HPC members got in and left. I waited with two other Afghans from HPC Joint Secretariat for the vehicle's return. But there was no sign of any vehicle coming back for us.

I said, let's walk outside base to a field where additional police trucks were parked. But these guys were afraid to walk the short distance, preferring to wait for a vehicle. I pointed out it was getting late, that I'd walk. I guess they were shamed into joining me, hardly keeping up with my long strides. They said they'd walk just as fast if they wore hiking shoes like me. I replied, "Doubtless!"

At the open field, people were waiting for us. We hopped into police Ford Ranger trucks for the half-hour ride to the governor's compound. These trucks were unarmored and without electronic countermeasures to remotely detonate roadside bombs. But their lack of safety paled in comparison to the Afghans' driving. I felt we'd either be in a head-on collision or end up in ravines and ditches. I kept asking the Khost HPC chair how much longer to get there. His response was always, "five minutes." After several "five minutes," we arrived safely at the provincial government compound.

Deputy Governor Abdul Wahid Patan told us the governor was in Kabul. After a few minutes of small talk with thirty people consisting of government personnel and tribal elders, we were led to the outside terrace for tea. I was surprised to see a very familiar face: Sardar Mohammad, an ANP general I had worked with in Kandahar when I served at KPRT. He was Kandahar police chief at the time, but had been replaced in 2010. He was Provincial Chief of Police in Khost at that time. He said he was much happier in Khost because he's a Pashtun from the east and therefore more at home there.

Morning teatime was more like breakfast with cheese, honey, marmalade, flat bread, and tea premade with milk and sugar. We rode to the ribbon-cutting ceremony in armored SUVs with the governor's security detail and a police convoy. Fortunately, that ride wasn't as hair-raising as the previous one.

Boys held placards declaring: "We want peace. We want schools." A three-boy choir sang an impromptu peace song. The HPC VP gave them money. The short ribbon was cut into pieces by several dignitaries anxious to get a piece of the action. Speeches were given. On the way to another government guesthouse for lunch, a detour took us to Khost University campus. We didn't exit our vehicles, but I was pleased to have a chance to see the campus. From base Camp Salerno we helicoptered back to Kabul. How Afghans would continue peace engagements with fellow Afghans after we leave was anyone's guess!

Another Week of Peace and Unity event took place in Kabul on September 19 with over fifteen hundred of my closest friends. Speakers included President Hamid Karzai, his Second Vice President Khalili, and other dignitaries. All glorified the late Rabbani and talked about peace. A notorious former warlord, Sayaf, talked about the sins of suicide bombers. He explained from an Islamic point of view a suicide bomber commits three damnable sins. The first was taking the lives of targets. The second was taking their own lives. The third was violating the trust of people who'd allowed them into their space, not thinking they were there to kill them. He cited verses from the Quran, sayings of the Prophet Mohammad, and other Islamic traditions. Sayaf was very convincing; but unfortunately, with the history of a brutal warlord, his message might not have carried much weight.

Karzai was subdued and detached; most of his speech was about Rabbani. It was very clear he gave so much support to these events because of political expediency. Unfortunately, people used the peace process as a political tool. He had plans for presidential elections in 2014, for which he needed support from Rabbani's political party (Jamiat). He was constitutionally barred from running a third term, but there was intense speculation his older brother might run.

On September 22, an international peace conference was held in Kabul's posh Serena Hotel. Participants came from neighboring countries and farther away, such as Lebanon, Turkey, and the United Kingdom. Two men from Northern Ireland involved in the peace negotiations leading to the Good Friday Accords flew in. The majority of Kabul's diplomatic corps were present—except for Americans. The US Embassy decided not to let anyone attend due to security concerns. Most likely, I was the only American. MG Hook went as well, but left after lunch.

First Afghan Vice President Marshal Fahim gave the opening speech—leaving no doubt in people's minds where he stood on peace. Fahim is a former warlord with an eighth-grade education who doesn't believe in working for peace with the Taliban. He and those like him think we should stay indefinitely in Afghanistan to beat the Taliban into submission—by force, of course—for peace!

Representatives from the international community, the European Union, the United Nations, and others talked about the importance of peace in Afghanistan, the region, and the world. But I found the best and most relevant speeches came from the Irishmen, Dennis Haughey and Jeffery Donaldson, which generated much discussion and comments. The Irishmen talked separately, but both echoed a common theme that they weren't there to tell Afghans how to achieve peace. Instead, how Afghans would achieve peace would be up to Afghans.

"We're here to tell you what worked for us. We're all children of God, therefore we should all work for peace," one said. They advised respecting the enemy, not agreeing on anything until everyone agreed on everything, and that any agreement should have the support of the people determined by a common referendum.

Many prominent Afghans in the audience (including a Kabul University professor) expressed contempt in talking to the Taliban because they've no regard for democracy, openness, and women's rights. They believed that the only way to achieve peace was to kill them off. The ugly professor rhetorically asked: "Peace at what price?"

Jeffery Donaldson, whose family members were killed by the Irish Republican Army, said people often ask, "Why do you talk to people who have done terrible things to you?" He replies, "For the future of our children." Peace was priceless. They advised on negotiation techniques such as having everything on the table, finding a way out for opponents, and other tips for peaceful negotiations. He offered this famous and immortal Irish prayer:

May the road rise up to meet you. May the wind always be at your back. May the sun shine warm upon your face and the rains fall soft upon your fields. And until we meet again, may the Lord hold your hand in His Hands.

Alas, many from the international community were very dismissive of the peace process. Only Ambassador Foley of Australia who'd been there three years and was about to depart understood what was going on. The German Deputy Chief of Mission thought he was an Afghanistan expert after arriving only two months before. The Norwegian ambassador was equally dismissive, seeing it as just a show.

Indeed, the road to peace in Afghanistan will be long, arduous, strewn with politically dangerous tribal/ethnic twists, and will mean literally going through very dangerous neighborhoods infused with some very ill-intentioned neighbors. I'm sure there are more obstacles I could mention.

But we have to start somewhere—or not go anywhere. Furthermore, all endeavors have both positive and negative sides to consider. There's no downside ever in working for peace, and there is reason enough to make every effort to start the peace journey. Achieving peace is not staging an event, but a p-r-o-c-e-s-s requiring adamantine determination, patience, and perseverance.

The last event of the Week of Peace was a conference organized by the Ulema Shura (Council of Clergy). I was the only ISAF person who attended. Unfortunately, the theme was very anticoalition and anti-West; burning the Qurans came up, as well as the derogatory video of Prophet Mohammed. The speakers were talking to their constituencies to gain political support. I hope they didn't incite large followings.

Here's a kicker. Even though US Embassy personnel were nowhere to be seen at these events, they became very busy writing cables based on other people's notes to show that they were doing something. I read some which were very slanted, so we didn't clear them. The other thing that ticked me off was their using my firsthand reports without attributing my observations. Such is life in a dog eat dog world of war and elusive peace!

MG Hook would leave soon and was busily making the rounds. I would be sorry to see him go. I very much appreciated his leadership style (see my picture with him in the photo gallery). I went with him to Regional Command North, close to the ancient city of Mazar-e-Sharif. There's no mistaking the base was built by Germans and efficiently run by them. Camp Marmal was the largest German military installation outside of Germany. The one-hour trip in a Citation executive jet was very comfortable. Clearly, the Germans worked hard. The German Bundeswehr's planes were parked precisely on the tarmac. VIP transient sleeping quarters were very clean, orderly, and complete with sheets, pillows, and comforters.

We were up early the next morning, held a few meetings, and were off to the neighboring province of Sar-e-Pul. It took forty-five minutes by Black Hawk helicopters. We met with the governor and officials from peace and reconciliation organizations. All complained about problems such as a lack of vehicles to get around; they asked us to bring their plight to the attention of Afghan authorities in Kabul. I told them this was an Afghan process, and they needed to pressure Kabul on it.

Around 11:30 a.m., we waited at the nearby dirt field for the choppers. We landed at Marmal on the nose at 12:30 p.m. for lunch. Our return flight to Kabul was delayed due to weather problems. We waited in a tent furnished with cushy couches and a few refrigerators full of drinks, including beer. (Go Germans!) US military camps in Afghanistan are dry, so seeing beer in Marmal was eye-popping and inviting.

There was snow on the higher peaks, the nights were crisp, and the days were very pleasant in Kabul at that time. And there were just a few more days before I flew home!

CHAPTER 14

11.21.2012:
Effective Leaders Must Be Determined Movers and Shakers

My two plus weeks at home flew by. As Yogi Berra quipped, "It is déjà vu all over again." I returned to my old ISAF room, to the upper bunk I'd occupied when I first arrived. Fortunately, ten days later, I was moved to a new building and to a two-person room.

Our new boss was Major General Edward Smyth-Osbourne, a cavalry officer of the United Kingdom. Whereas with our previous director, MG Hook, we worked toward handing over more responsibility to Afghans in transitioning out—this new guy wanted to be involved in everything anew!

This was a big challenge our mission in Afghanistan faced. We reinvented the wheel every time a new chief came on board. By the time the new chief learned the tricks of the trade and got to know his Afghan counterparts, it was time to leave. MG Hook took ten months to get to know the character of Stanakzai, Joint Secretariat head. All that knowledge was gone. Afghans were well aware of this weakness and took full advantage of playing the new guy.

British Major General Nick Carter, whom I'd worked with during my deployment in Kandahar, had been Commander of Regional Command South, which included Kandahar, as well as Zabul and Neimroz Provinces. With an extra star on his shoulder, LTG Carter returned as ISAF Deputy Commander.

The mission in Afghanistan was a revolving door; people come, go back, get promoted, and return there to a bigger job. However, this cycle would be broken with the next commander. Marine General Joseph Dunford replaced General John Allen in February 2013. General Dunford, a logistics specialist, didn't have prior Afghanistan experience, which meant he didn't carry any Afghan-related emotional baggage. He was therefore uniquely positioned to drastically reduce our involvement in Afghanistan.

It was difficult to get back to work due to jet lag, my bunk situation, and the US presidential elections, which was a huge source of distraction in the offices. Wide-screen TVs were tuned to different channels depending on people's political inclinations, from people on the right of Attila the Hun to moderates, liberals, and progressives. It was interesting the entire fabric of American politics was represented here, half a world away.

Conservatives were extremely giddy in the run up to the elections as they continually reinforced their belief the polls were biased—except for FOX TV's projections. Liberals were emotionally wound up in reflecting their liberally biased polls. At 3:30 a.m. on November 7 (6:00 p.m. EST, November 6), Steve, a DOD civilian, watched voting returns in the office. When I arrived at 7:30 a.m., his mood was grim, especially when FOX gave Ohio to Obama. Then his mood brightened some when Karl Rove tried in vain to push back, but FOX number-crunchers stood their ground.

Ginger, a USAF colonel sharing an office with Steve, was very nervous, even as Obama seemed to surge ahead. Although Ginger isn't a one-issue person, a lot was riding for her on Obama's reelection. Ginger and Steve constantly screamed at each other, loudly reverberating throughout the whole floor.

Before the repeal of "Don't Ask, Don't Tell," and even in 2012, there're many who believe gays shouldn't serve openly in the military. Their reason is that it adversely affects morale and unit cohesion. A coworker from Virginia was gay, in her midforties, and with a partner of eleven years. She headed operations in overseeing eight military officers of varying ranks and nationalities. She was on the move constantly, engaging Afghans at HPC's Joint Secretariat, which has operational responsibilities. I worked very closely with her and can testify she stands shoulder to shoulder relative to her leadership skills and can-do attitude with any man or woman, gay or straight. Another gay woman, a colonel, is equally competent. At least in these two cases with which I'm very familiar, sexual orientation doesn't have bearings on people's professional conduct.

Professional conduct is a hot topic these days in Washington and here in Afghanistan!

I thought I was having a bad dream when I saw headlines announcing General Petraeus's resignation because of his extramarital affair with his biographer-admirer. We were just warming up to the scandal when the other shoe dropped. It was reported General Allen had e-mail communications with Jill Kelley, a woman at the heart of this scandal. I hoped Allen's e-mails were innocuous enough that he would come out unscathed. But what will be, will be, que sera, sera. Even the most admired military officer is a human being embedded with human frailties. The problem? We're perennially so consumed with making demigods of human beings we forget even the gods fall too.

That being said, people in positions like Petraeus's have more obligations than just to their families. They've obligations to the country. They should, therefore, be constantly mindful of staying clear of questionable personal indulgences. I'm not passing judgment as to their personal conduct, but their actions do directly affect our mission in Afghanistan—and by extension, our country. This provokes Afghans to ask: How can people with such bad judgment do their job properly, and how can they make the right decisions for the mission to succeed in Afghanistan?

Unfortunately, I had to answer these questions when I worked with Afghans as a bridge-builder between them and us. More importantly, since Karzai and others blamed most ills befalling Afghanistan on the United States, such incidents provided ammo for them. The Taliban had already started poking fun, not only at Petraeus, but at all Americans. Incidents like these play right into the hands of people who wish us ill.

Amid the brouhaha, there was some good news. An HPC delegation went to Pakistan. It was a good trip, resulting in Pakistan releasing some Taliban. Pakistan had detained a number of Taliban over the years. The reason was not because Pakistan had a falling out with these Taliban; the

Taliban were arrested for being open to negotiations with Karzai's government or because they were no longer useful to Pakistan.

It was difficult to gauge the Pakistan government's intentions at that point, but it was nonetheless a positive step. I was particularly happy Chairman Rabbani, who I advised and mentored, did very well in leading this delegation. Just two days before the delegation left, I had helped edit a plan for the discussions that would take place.

This successful trip took many skeptics by surprise, especially because detainees were released. The joint communiqué issued after the trip was promising, as well. Both sides called on insurgents to lay down arms and to join the Afghan Peace and Reconciliation Program. They also recommended organizing religious conferences to push along the peace process to encourage insurgents to sever all ties to Al-Qaeda.

At the top of the list of those released was Mullah Turabi, Minister of Justice during the Taliban regime. He was personally responsible for establishing a very brutal system to enforce Taliban laws. Methods the Taliban used included stoning adulterers to death, cutting off the hands of thieves, and punishing men whose beards were not long enough. In March 2001, he had a big hand in blowing up fifteen-hundred-year-old Bamiyan Buddha statues, including a 180-foot-tall statue, in central Afghanistan. How a person of his mentality can become peaceful remained an open question. We didn't know where these people would end up or what roles they would play in the peace process.

I tried to go to HPC offices three times weekly, depending on Rabbani's travel schedule and other events. What was amazing was the lack of urgency on the part of Afghans. I typically arrived at 9:00 a.m. and found myself the first one there. Around 9:30 a.m., people started trickling in. Their routine started with drinking tea, socializing, and maybe squeezing some business in between. They broke for lunch around noon, and most were gone by 3:30 p.m.

Most Afghans were so accustomed to the status quo, the situation seemed normal to them. Even worse were Afghans with dual citizenships who returned owing to family or other connections. These mostly inept people were paid by international organizations and earned many times more than the average Afghan. They were in no hurry to help Afghanistan; the longer the situation lingered, the more financially beneficial for them, of course.

On November 17, we planned another visit to Khost—with the Governor of Khost, a member of HPC, Qamar Khosti, and an Afghan with a dual passport, Aziz. We were at a nearby base for our helicopter ride at 8:00 a.m. But due to inclement weather, we waited until noon for the next attempt to fly out. MG Smyth-Osbourne told the Afghans he'd devoted the whole day for this trip, so he was willing to wait it out.

But Aziz tried his hardest to cancel the trip, telling other Afghans they wouldn't accomplish anything by waiting. While we were trying to engage the governor and HPC member Qamar to find out about their issues, Aziz was busy with his phones texting and talking. What a commitment to solving Afghanistan's problems! At 12:00 we took off, flew half an hour, landed halfway to refuel, and returned to Kabul as the weather worsened. Aziz got his wish because of bad weather. There we were, trying to connect Afghans at great expense while accepting personal risks—and Aziz didn't want to inconvenience himself!

On Wednesday, November 21, I came to the office all "duded up" in coat and tie to attend a meeting with the general and HPC chair at their offices. An hour before, we heard an explosion outside HQ ISAF, so the entire camp went into lockdown mode. An IED had hit one of our ISAF vehicles; fortunately no one was injured. Lockdown was lifted at 10:00 a.m., and we continued with our program.

Since the destroyed ISAF Land Cruiser was one of two in which the general travels, his security detail scrambled to find another vehicle on short notice. We left camp in a two-vehicle convoy, but couldn't get out of Green Zone. So we returned to HQ ISAF and left from the back gate that opened out onto a street outside. We were a bit late for the meeting, but ended up having a very good meeting. HPC Chair Rabbani was upbeat about his upcoming trip to Pakistan—which, as I described above, was a huge success.

Later, I learned two suicide bombers had tried to get into Green Zone. They were stopped at the checkpoint manned by Afghan police. When the bombers noticed the ISAF vehicle approaching, one set off his vest packed with steel ball bearings. It damaged the armored SUV and killed his cohort before he was able to set off his other bomb. Unfortunately, two policemen were also killed and a few civilians injured.

On Thanksgiving, we had plans to fly to a northwestern province, Badghis, but it was canceled, so we had turkey instead! I learned at that time that General Allen had returned to Kabul and resumed command; I was glad of that good news!

CHAPTER 15

12.19.2012:
Preparing to Draw Down Peacefully from Afghanistan

November 24 was a day of heightened security. The year before on that day, a suicide bomber had detonated his explosive-lined vest in a Shia (or Shiite) mosque in Kabul, killing fifty people and injuring scores more. The attacker couldn't have targeted a better day to inflict the most carnage. Shia mosque Takia Khana was located in an old part of Kabul, Murad Khani, and was at overflowing capacity with worshipers commemorating "Ashura."

At the daily morning stand up meeting on November 24, I was asked to describe the significance of Ashura and whether there'd be problems that day. There were reports of potential bombings, but I wasn't in a position to predict what might happen. I did, however, give a bit of Ashura's history and significance.

Ashura (meaning "tenth" in Arabic) is celebrated on the tenth day of the first month of the Islamic calendar, Muharram. Since the Islamic calendar is based on the lunar cycle, it moves ten days per year relative to the solar-based Gregorian calendar.

Muharram is one of four holy months of the Islamic year. Muslims observe Ashura to commemorate the freedom of Israelites from Egyptian pharaohs. Prophet Mohammad fasted during Ashura to observe this day. Also on this day the Prophet's grandson, Husain, was massacred with seventy of his companions in Karbala, in Iraq. He's revered by Shias as the hidden righteous Imam who they believe will one day reappear.

Shias go through self-flagellation rituals and other forms of self-punishment to reenact Husain's martyrdom and suffering. Many whip their backs using chains with small razor-like extensions and end up bleeding profusely. The Sunnis observe the day by fasting and giving alms or food to the poor. This year, the grand Shia mullah (priest) in Kabul told adherents to donate blood instead of wasting it. President Karzai, a Sunni, and other high Afghan officials went to a blood bank to give blood—obviously a very positive development in an otherwise senseless religious ritual.

Although there were no incidents similar to the previous year's carnage, a dispute broke out at Kabul University between the two religious camps. Shia students wanted to hold a service in the mosque, which Sunnis opposed, resulting in fighting. Several students were injured and one died. This was very disturbing because, at least in theory, a university is a place of learning, tolerance, understanding, and peaceful debate. To contain any further escalation of violence, the authorities cancelled classes for a few days.

Our new FRI-C director, MG Smyth-Osbourne had a very intense travel schedule that kept most of us on our toes. From November 27 to 29, we covered most of the north provinces in three days at dizzying pace. We left in the morning from Kabul to Mazar-e-Sharif in a Belgium military transport plane and upon arrival, transferred to a German transporter to Kunduz. We were driven to the German Provincial Reconstruction Team (PRT) compound about five minutes away in a Bundeswehr armored vehicle. After a quick lunch, we boarded two German helicopters and flew to Baghlan PRT in the capital, Pul-e-Khumri. Baghlan PRT was run by the Bulgarians. We met with the PRT commander and then with Afghan provincial, security, and peace committee officials.

We scurried back to the helipad (a dirt strip of land by the river) when we heard the German choppers approaching, kicking up dust and other debris as they descended. Forty minutes later, we were back at the Kunduz PRT. We were assigned rooms for the night. Meticulous German planning and organization were at work everywhere: from well-built, clean, and orderly barracks, to the dining facility (DFAC) that was a cut above others (although unsurprisingly, pork products dominated the menu).

We were honestly quite surprised to find this singular DFAC manned by German personnel and run by the Bundeswehr. In contrast, other DFACs in Afghanistan were run by companies staffed with the cheapest labor from India, the Philippines, and other non-Europeans. Another advantage of a German facility was beer and wine available in the evenings. After dinner, we headed to the Weinstube with a two-beer limit per person or a bottle of wine for three. Luckily, these military bartenders weren't very fussy about keeping count. I was sure this didn't matter to the camp residents, but for people like us from high and dry camps, it was a big deal. Of course we indulged; even our boss, MG Ed, joined in the next night!

We woke up early the next day to pouring rain. Someone said it hadn't rained in five months. We had a full day of meetings in Kunduz in the morning and at neighboring Takhar in the afternoon. Folks in Takhar complained they didn't have vehicles, salaries weren't paid on time, and there was a general lack of support from central Afghan authorities in Kabul. No surprise!

At the end of the day, we realized we didn't have any euros left to party again at the Weinstube. Worse, the money exchange hut had closed. So I went to the German Post Exchange to buy a few trinkets with large bills and got the change back in Euros. Our evening festivities resumed!

We usually took Afghan officials with us when we traveled to the provinces. On this trip, we had an NDS liaison colonel with us. NDS was responsible for vetting insurgents who chose to lay down arms to rejoin their communities.

Afghans who traveled with us had to find accommodations outside our bases. They were to show up at 8:00 a.m. the next morning for the trip back to Kabul. But because of inclement weather, the morning flight was cancelled. They arrived at the prescribed time but waited a long time. When they finally got access inside the PRT to join us, it was almost noon. The German DFAC was off limits for Afghans, which was very strange.

Colonel Ezatullah (a short, stocky diabetic) was usually affable, but a combination of waiting so long at the gate and not eating lunch had made him very cranky. No sooner had I sat next to him than he started complaining. He was irate, saying he wasn't anyone's servant and that the Americans should respect him, otherwise he'd stop cooperating.

Yet again, I was caught between both sides as a "peace bridge-builder." The colonel didn't speak any English; he told me I understood his situation better because I'm Afghan. I tried to explain no one meant any disrespect and that it was all an unfortunate misunderstanding. After assuring him I'd talk to everyone including the general about the issue and apologizing profusely, he calmed down. This situation was a good example of another challenge for us that required constant attention and diplomatic mindfulness.

An announcement told us to get ready for the airport as there was a flight leaving for Mazar-e-Sharif, but without guarantee of a connecting flight to Kabul. German armored vehicles took us to the airfield where we boarded a Norwegian air force C130 to Mazar. This later version of the C130 was testimony to Norway's wealth. A half-hour later we arrived. The back ramp dropped down; a German officer got on to announce that MG Smyth-Osbourne's party would deplane first. A bus took us about a hundred yards to another military transport for the flight back to Kabul.

There was lots of talk then about reorganization at HQ ISAF. Personnel would be reduced. The idea was to transition over to Afghan authorities as we entered the New Year. This was a good move as this HQ had been extremely bloated, regardless of the transition phase. There were many people there that no one knew what to do with. With a rampant lack of accountability, no one was asked about what and how they were contributing to the mission.

Furthermore, people were afraid to hear the truth! I was asked to prepare a presentation on HPC (where I was embedded) and an assessment of the chair's job. The night before my presentation to ISAF Commander I shared it with my boss, MG Smyth-Osbourne who told me that it was "too honest;" therefore it shouldn't be shared in the forum presentation. I refused to change the tone or content of what I had stated. I would offer it unfiltered for all the time I'd been doing this job. For obvious reasons, no one there was more qualified than me to produce a realistic review of what was happening. How were we to make "right decisions" and influence events if we didn't understand problems? I kept asking myself this, but hadn't been able to answer my own question adequately.

Many people there were careful not to be blunt with high-level Afghan officials because they were afraid it'd undermine their relationships. But I felt that we needed to hold the Afghans responsible for working for their country. My argument was that we built relationships to support the mission, not the other way around. If a relationship couldn't support and help sustain the mission, then we should've changed it. If this mission succeeded, it'd be good for Afghans, the entire region, the United States, and the whole world.

Failure though would have the opposite effect and dire consequences. I didn't think one had to be a rocket scientist to understand this straightforward, simple concept. Sadly, no one acknowledged we'd become enablers of some good, but mostly of the bad and the ugly, Afghan dudes who'd no interest in the success of this mission.

I'd wanted to meet with President Karzai for the past three months. But due to his busy schedule, we hadn't been able to. One day, from out of the blue, my friend from the palace called to say the president wanted to see me in the next few days if I was available. My response was that of course, I'd make myself available any time. On December 5, he called for me to come over Friday for lunch. I got permission from my boss. On the sixth, the Afghan Spy Chief was wounded by a suicide bomber—which I thought might complicate my meeting. I was ready to be picked up at 12:30 p.m. on Friday the seventh when I received a call that the president's schedule had abruptly changed. Our meeting was rescheduled for the same time on Saturday the eighth.

On Saturday, a nondescript white Toyota Corolla picked me up at 12:45 p.m. for a two-minute trip dotted with checkpoints en route to the palace. After security, a person from the palace protocol said the president would perform the early afternoon prayer first.

He escorted me to the palace's old ornate mosque, but the president wasn't there. Since there were others ready to pray, I took off my shoes and joined in. I didn't remember when the last time was I'd prayed in a mosque. Although I'd showered, I didn't go through the ritual of washing private parts, hands, feet, and face that's required before daily prayers. Once the mullah started the prayers, I realized I was rusty in reciting certain passages of the Quran and other readings. I essentially partially faked it. I was definitely headed straight to hell afterward!

It took six minutes to complete the prayers. Outside, people were waiting to take me to the small palace, Gul Khana, a solarium. This was the building that had been King Zahir Shah's winter office. I waited in the large waiting room. Then I heard President Karzai come down from his second-floor office. We went to the hallway at the bottom of the grand staircase where he greeted me very warmly with an embrace.

I followed him to the grand dining room. There were five place settings on the huge dining table. He took his usual seat at the head of the table and told me to sit on his right. His National Security Advisor, Spanta, and his deputy sat opposite me, while Karzai's personal physician took a seat to my right.

Lunch consisted of "mashawa," a delicious thick lentil soup of spices and yogurt; a spinach dish; another lentil dish; rice pilaf with nuts, raisins, and julienned carrots; whole wheat Afghan flat bread or naan; salad; delicious fruit; Afghan custard pudding for desert; and green tea. The most important treat was a glass of ruby red, freshly squeezed Kandahar pomegranate juice. How many pomegranates for a glass? One large pomegranate!

I did most of the talking, which consisted of briefing the president on the status of the Peace and Reintegration Program. I explained to him the deficiencies, what needed fixing, and who was responsible. I didn't shy away from being "too honest."

We discussed many other issues, and he was very appreciative of my candor. He took notes and directed the Deputy National Security Advisor to organize meetings with the relevant people. The plan was for me to join him in his office for a one-on-one meeting following lunch, but someone slipped him a note which changed the schedule. He invited me to come back another time.

I waited for my photograph with President Karzai taken by the palace photographer to arrive. Personal cameras were not allowed for security reasons.

Meeting the president of a country is a big deal—especially for a grunt like me to receive unhindered access. But did anyone care? Nope. I wrote a report after my meeting with President Karzai, but no one asked any questions, asked my impressions about him, or anything. I was really surprised by the lack of interest.

The weather had gotten considerably colder, ranging from high teens to the low twenties at night, and midthirties during the day. The first season's snow fell on Kabul then, although the surrounding mountains were already capped with the white stuff a month before. On December 24, I left for Paris and Dusseldorf to see my sisters and mother, then had ten days of R&R at home.

CHAPTER 16

2.1.2013:
Final Impressions

Returning from R&R to a medium-security prison was always a bit of a challenge due to jet lag, poor living conditions, and especially at this time of year, going from 85 degrees Fahrenheit to snow and subfreezing temperatures. Snow is nice, but there the enjoyment was limited to the visual effects when I occasionally peeked out at the surrounding white peaks through the makeshift structures at headquarters.

That time, the readjustment was easier as I was entering the final stretch! My tour was ending by the end of February. Sadly though, it was clearly a different feeling from what I felt at the end of my first tour in January 2011.

I left the private sector in 2009 to serve and to contribute to what I then considered the most important foreign policy and national security challenge facing the United States. Stakes for the country of my birth, Afghanistan, were even higher. I felt a profound duty to repay the debts I owed Afghanistan and my adopted country, America. Ultimately, what I stand for today has been shaped by these two countries.

Although as individuals we're insignificant in the grand cosmic design, we can still dream of making a difference, personally. Our contributions can be significant in cooperation with others, in synergy with a system that provides for, and encourages, teamwork. Functional synergy requires constituent parts to be precisely designed to coexist as cohesively as possible for our actions to be successful—or else we face dysfunctional entropy.

When I joined the US Department of State to begin my first tour, I was initially slated for Marjah, a restive district of Helmand Province, which at the time was still in the hands of the Taliban. But by chance, I ran into then Deputy Chief of Mission Tony Wayne at the US Embassy in Kabul who recognized my skill set was better suited for Kandahar. Tony Wayne had become US ambassador to Mexico since then; he had the power to make things happen, and they worked out as well as I'd imagined and hoped for.

In contrast, when I arrived in Kabul at the beginning of my second tour in March 2012, I was sent to a training center for three weeks for a crash course in Afghan culture and languages! I informed the acting program head that, being a native speaker, I needed no such training and to instead put me to more productive work. But he didn't have the authority to make an exception—nor did he bother to check with his superiors.

It took me four long months of lobbying and prodding to join an organization where I could be a force multiplier. Although going to FRI-C to work on peace issues was an improvement, I was still misplaced in achieving the productivity I wanted for our mission. It's hard to come up with reasons to explain why there were such marked differences between my two tours of duty. Perhaps one was that in Kandahar, we were at the frontline—which affected people's organizational and personal behaviors differently in instilling a sense of urgency. Perhaps it was a cosmic combination of time, place, and people coming together in happy serendipity and synergy.

At HQ ISAF, most saw other people as competition, thus forgetting we were all there for the bigger purpose of serving the mission. In Kandahar, most of us had tried hard to move forward, commensurate with other parts of our professional machinery. That attitude and behavior also brought us closer together and generated an atmosphere of unprecedented camaraderie. The added benefit was that it minimized organizational distractions and enabled a collective focus on our mission.

In December 2009, President Barack Obama announced, in a major speech at West Point, our military surge and involvement in Afghanistan. I for one enthusiastically supported the surge as it would finally focus on the restive south and greater Kandahar area (and Helmand). The British in Helmand and Canadians in Kandahar didn't have sufficient resources to keep insurgents out of their major districts. I also figured we'd have learned much in nine years there by way of economic development and building capacity; meaning, business as usual in the old ways would have changed.

We were, therefore, encouraged to do whatever it took to make things happen—by changing the status quo to help Afghans rebuild on a new foundation. We used tactics such as (1) putting matters within the Afghan context, (2) listening to Afghans about their priorities, (3) not channeling aid through NGOs, and (4) discontinuing support of warlords and other corrupt powerbrokers. Three years later in 2012, we were half-heartedly talking about disengagement and transition.

I had, however, also come to the conclusion we should disengage from Afghanistan. Why? What I thought might have occurred by early 2013 in terms of security and Afghans taking responsibility for their country had not materialized.

Too, while talking of transitioning, many people had a hard time letting go. Why? Because letting go is inconsistent with military mentality because it's admitting defeat.

But to me, making Afghans responsible while we were still there, to step back some and help out as needed, would ensure things wouldn't totally collapse at the end of 2014, when we finally ceased much of our involvement. We needed to take the training wheels off and let them stumble a bit. If they were about to fall, then we'd extend our arms to maintain their balance. This would help them learn to ride the bike with minor bruises, but we'd still be there to hold them in case they fell off.

Back in August 2012, I sent my then boss MG Hook an e-mail with the subject line title, "Smart Transition." The following is a redacted version:

MG Hook,

Following our meeting yesterday about giving the Afghans more responsibility, I would like to share my thoughts with you.

We should take an inventory of our tasks in various areas of our involvement and divide them into branches to be handed over to our Afghan counterparts between now and the end of 2014. We can assess which ones can be handed over first without severely affecting the program. Hence Smart Transition…

He replied:
Abdullah,
"This idea has merit and is worthy of careful consideration."

He then ordered his Chief of Staff Colonel Mark Manwaring to organize a team discussion to come up with a "way forward plan." Post-discussion, a proposal was presented. But six months later, we hadn't handed over even one task to the Afghans, who were happy with the status quo. High-ranking Afghan officials we dealt with were happy, because the more we did, the less they had to do!

In November 2011, I was invited to address the members of the First Marine Expeditionary Force before their deployment to Afghanistan. Their commander, MG Gurganus, asked how he could get his marines out of Afghanistan as soon as possible. I replied it was very simple: the more the Afghans do, the less your marines will have to and the sooner Afghans step up to the plate, the sooner your marines get out of Helmand. Time was well spent getting Afghans involved and pushing them to take responsibility for their country!

Another problem was that a majority of high-level government servants were incompetent, corrupt, unpatriotic, egotistical, controlling, and masters at playing off and manipulating foreigners—to mention a few. Helping and empowering them was counterproductive. Truthfully, we had enabled them to diminish our efforts!

An incident in Kandahar in 2009 illustrates this point. We were lunching at KPRT chow hall. I noticed two air conditioners next to each other blasting away at top power. One was in the hot mode, while the other was pumping out cold air. Light bulb! One working against the other; this was what we'd been doing in Afghanistan! I so hoped we'd stop supporting the bad people! Alas, not much had changed.

Our new director at FRI-C, MG Ed, was busily travelling around the country reinventing the wheel without any focus on getting the transition moving forward. I sensed he was tired of my bringing up the subject every chance I got, but I would not give up! I was sure he'd be relieved when I left.

I had seen this mentality with some other British general officers. With their ancestors' past involvements in Afghanistan, which ended in 1919, some Brits think they're experts in everything Afghan. And while it's very important to be conscious of what happened in the past, it'd be total folly to apply these events directly to the present.

Both present and past are constrained by different time, space, social, geopolitical, societal, and myriad other conditions. Any lesson learned from history needs to be modified to current constraints to have any chance of producing relevant effects. But in a military hierarchy, which is a very blunt instrument for solving nonmilitary problems, it's hopeless when the boss decides everything without getting input from others with more ground experience in solving nonmilitary problems.

Governance and diplomacy are truly, wholly different beasts, altogether!

No one on their own can ever hope to solve Afghan problems--except Afghans. This is generally the case regardless of location. Its true Afghanistan's challenges are profound and the following country examples may not apply, but one can still make the case for relevant, appropriate procedures.

For instance, as the United States helped Europe regain its feet in the aftermath of World War II, the Europeans themselves were the primary forces expending their own efforts to rebuild with The Marshall Plan. South Korea's another good example. Those of us helping Afghans transition needed to constantly think about this in our daily operations, but more often than not, it was hardly on the radar.

The United States had spent $606 billion ($606,000,000,000) in Afghanistan by February 2013. At $300 million per day, this figure increased significantly from there. This translated to roughly $20,000 for every child, man, and woman in the United States over the previous eleven years. At the same time, the estimated per capita income in Afghanistan was $580 per year. If we'd given half this money directly to the Afghans, perhaps the situation could've been different; although I'm not being very serious in saying this, it's something to think about.

It didn't have to be this way, had we engaged the "right Afghans" in the "right way" at the "right time" during the past decade. By the way, we'd also spent $810 billion in Iraq by the same time, with the clock still ticking.

My last day in Afghanistan was scheduled for February 20. But it would take a few days to get home. I would depart Kabul for Kuwait for a Freedom Flight on February 23, which takes demobilizing folks to Camp Atterbury in Indiana. I'd have to turn in the useless stuff I was issued and process out, which would take another two days, and then finally I could fly home. Freedom Flights are operated by charter companies flying the oldest, most decrepit airplanes matched with lousy service. But hey, coming home would negate all that.

Before leaving, I was to write an evaluation of my tour to be signed off by my boss. I was having a difficult time doing it as there wasn't much I'd accomplished or contributed this time round. Colleagues told me to write whatever comes to mind as it doesn't matter; people even wrote up their own recommendations for medals (and they got them!).

Once home, I'd take a few weeks to decompress and readjust to a different reality. I would then report for a new assignment at Central Command in Tampa, Florida, which has overall responsibility for the Middle East and Afghanistan. I'd be moving again, but to a place with a shorter commute.

PS: The Pentagon's report on General Allen absolved him of any impropriety for the twenty thousand e-mails he sent to a Tampa woman who had brought down General Petraeus. I was glad he didn't get into trouble, because I respect and like him. His last day in Afghanistan was February 10. At the Change of Command ceremony, he'd pass the baton to General Dunford who, like Allen, was a four-star marine officer. General Dunford had no prior Afghan experience and was a logistics specialist. Perhaps we'd reduce our involvement in Afghanistan sooner and more substantially.

CHAPTER 17

3.15.2013:
My Second Tour in Afghanistan Ends

February 18, 2013, began like any other day. I woke up at 5:00 in the morning, went to the gym, took a shower, went to the chow hall for my last breakfast, and arrived at the office at 7:00 a.m. to watch the ISAF commander's morning meeting via secure video feed. At 8:00 a.m. we assembled at the FRI-C's conference room for our daily meeting with the Director, MG Ed Smyth-Osbourne. I said my farewells to my colleagues. MG Ed gave a speech full of praise, which was nice of him to do. A buffet of goodies was setup in the corridor for people to socialize in my honor. Around noon I was taken to the Kabul Airfield with our administration officer, Kelly, who was coming back to the United States for R&R. He was designated as my "plus one" or my handler because my GS-15 rank entitled me to certain privileges, at least in theory. I found out once again quickly that it was all in theory!

Upon arrival at Kabul International Airport (KAIA) North, we went to the office for our helicopter flight to Bagram Air Field, the staging place for our flight out of the country. KAIA North was under the control of ISAF and also housed the ISAF's Joint Command. KAIA South was under the control of Afghan authorities handling all civilian and some Afghan military flights. Flights were coordinated by contract personnel working for some war profiteer company. Most of these people were very rude as they had no accountability and they also realized that people were at their mercy. So, if one wanted service, one needed to kowtow to them. I found out that I was not on the flight manifest and had to wait another day. Kelly on the other hand was on the manifest and took off for Bagram later that day.

I had to go to the billeting office to find a place to sleep and wait for the next day. I found a bed in a room equipped with multiple bunk beds, but fortunately it was not too crowded. I could not haul all of my heavy gear consisting of body armor and other things, which I had to return to the United States. So I left them by the air terminal on an outdoor rack hoping that they would not be stolen by the time my flight left for Bagram, whenever that would be. The next day I made several trips to the flight line to find out the time to leave. It was very frustrating to be uncertain. I had to be in Bagram early on the twentieth to make the flight to Kuwait, to make my way home. As the evening approached, they finally told me I was scheduled to leave at 3:00 on February 20. After dinner, I went back to the flight line and waited until the wee hours of the morning. The flight was delayed, but I finally arrived in Bagram around 5:00.

I was directed to go to a huge hanger to get the details for the Kuwait flight later that day. I was able to find Kelly who was also waiting. It was a chaotic scene with contractors, soldiers, and others who were returning home for good, for R&R, or for other reasons. Several hours later we were told to go to an adjacent hanger for security screening. There was already a huge line, so more waiting was required. I used the time to throw out some of my belongings and was able to consolidate my stuff into two duffel bags and a roller bag. After the security screening, we were sequestered anew for another two hours or so. I was very tired and hungry. At the VIP (that was what it was called, but it was anything but a VIP lounge) waiting area. Fortunately the VIP lounge was stocked with water and MRE packages, which came in very handy. An announcement jolted us from the boredom of waiting. We were bussed to the flight line where a USAF behemoth C17 Globemaster transport plane was waiting for us. I took a seat in the front row. The engines came to life, the plane rolled onto the runway, and soon it was airborne. The C17 is designed for short takeoff and landings using unpaved runways for the delivery of troops and war equipment near battlefields in less than ideal conditions. It is also designed as a strategic airlift platform, for transporting personnel and equipment throughout the world.

Approximately three hours later, we landed at the Ali Al Salem Airbase in Kuwait where I first arrived in March of the previous year for my deployment to Afghanistan. This time I knew the routine better. I went to the billeting to get a bed and the other things I needed. We had to wait for two days before flying back to the United States on a chartered civilian airplane. Once again, on the day of the flight we had to go through security screening, sequestration, and the whole process. To my dismay, I found out that it was a contractor flight and I was not a distinguished visitor (DV), which would have allowed me to board first and get a good seat. But it did not really matter as the plane was not full to capacity. I found a middle row all to myself where I stretched as I wished.

The first stop was Shannon, Ireland, where a pint of Guinness along with a smoked salmon sandwich on my favorite Irish brown soda bread hit the spot! We arrived in Indianapolis in the morning of February 23. Our final destination for demobilization was Camp Atterbury, about a half-hour drive from Indianapolis. While everyone else waited for military busses, I rented a car to have more flexibility and to be able leave as soon as possible. I brought Kelly along, and we left the airport for the camp. On the way, we stopped at a Bob Evans restaurant for some greasy breakfast. Once at the camp, I went directly to the warehouse to get rid of my assigned stuff, most of which I did not use during my deployment. I then proceeded to medical checkup, which included some sort of psychological test to make sure I had not gone insane!

Although I had braced myself for a stay of several days there, I was able to complete the paperwork in one day. The next day, I had a plane ticket for my trip home to Florida. The rental car came in handy as there was not official transport available for the trip back to the Indianapolis airport. Kelly came with me and, since I did not have much time, I dropped myself at the curb and asked him to return the rental car. I was elated to make the nonstop flight back to Fort Myers. My plan was to take a few days off before beginning my assignment at Central Command (CENTCOM) in Tampa. It was great to be home!

CHAPTER 18

5.10.2014
My Stint at CENTCOM

As I explained in chapter 1, I am a part of the AfPak program with multiple deployments to Afghanistan, with in between assignments in the United States in a military organization. When I came back home I expected to begin my assignment at CENTCOM no later than April 2013. I needed a higher level security clearance, which came through, but there was no sign of any orders from the army to go to CENTCOM. People at CENTCOM were eager for me to start my job there, but nothing was happening. March flew by, April came and went, May, June, nothing. In the meantime, I was not being paid, but my health insurance continued as before. The traffic of the myriad e-mails was astounding, but there was no result. Once again, it was the bureaucracy at work. Apparently the army bean counters did not care whether I worked or not.

The month of June went by quickly, and one day toward the end of July, I received a confusing email with an attached form to be immediately completed for the release of my orders to start at CENTCOM. Four wasted months! I sprang into action and went to Tampa to find a place to live, all at my own expense, another benefit of being a civilian in the military. Perhaps the Civilian Expeditionary Force does not have the same priority as the real personnel. While waiting for my paperwork, I did not receive my salary. So I had to wage an exhausting battle royal with the army bureaucracy to get my back pay. I was victorious at the end, but I wish I did not have to go through it.

The US Central Command, which was established in 1983, is located at MacDill Air Force Base in Tampa, Florida. Its area of responsibility

(AOR) consists of about twenty countries in the Middle East and Central Asia, in addition to Afghanistan and Pakistan. CENTCOM has the overall responsibility for all US military engagement activities, planning, and operations in its AOR.

I began my assignment at CENTCOM's Plans Division of the Strategy, Policy, and Plans Directorate (J5). The J5 provides input into and translates national-level strategies, policies, and plans into strategic-operational level long-range guidance. It also leads the overarching Campaign and Strategic Planning Process. It integrates interagency and command efforts toward the attainment of the command's vision, goals, and objectives. The CENTCOM J5 has subject matter expertise and country insight on all military and political aspects for the region.

My group consisted of about ten officers and one civilian (me) working on plans for Afghanistan as the draw down of US and coalition forces was looming on the horizon. Disengagement at such a large scale is not a simple matter. All plans for the next phase of our involvement depended on the bilateral security agreement with the Government of Afghanistan. As the negotiations with Karzai dragged on, an undue burden was put on the plans division to come up with different scenarios covering possible contingencies. There were numerous meetings every day most of which consisted of summarizing plans into PowerPoint presentations for the higher ups. The meetings drew resources (military and civilian) from other groups as well. For me the whole thing was a drag because the effort was military planning in general with very little input from me, an expert on Afghanistan. In one of the meetings, a marine colonel estimated the salary of the people in the meeting to be over $1 million, yet we were all working on a PowerPoint presentation design. His point was that spending all this money to just produce a presentation might horrify the taxpayer.

One day we received an email from the commander's office asking for any input on the commander's briefing book as he was going to travel to Afghanistan where he would meet with Karzai. Since I was probably the only one at CENTCOM who had actually met with Karzai and was very familiar with the issues, I thought I could make a good contribution by meeting with the commander, General Lloyd Austin. So I sent an email back in response to the request numerating the issues in the hope of getting a brief invitation to elaborate and prepare the commander. But, to my surprise there was no such interest in the commander's office! I did, however, receive an email saying that they would include my points in the briefing book.

As time went by, I realized there was not much use for me in the plans division, so I tried to go somewhere more suitable. I moved to Combined Strategic Analysis Group (CSAG), another division reporting to J5 directorate. CSAG hosted officers from many European and other countries. They were divided in groups covering CENTCOM's AOR. I was kind of a freelancer giving opinions on different matters, but writing analysis papers on Afghanistan. CSAG was headed by an Australian commodore, the equivalent of a vice admiral or a one-star general. The job of CSAG was to provide alternative opinions on matters concerning the countries in the AOR. I actually enjoyed my time there as I felt I was being productive.

In January 2014 I received word from the Pakistan Afghanistan Coordination Center at the Pentagon that the AfPak program was going to come to an end soon for the civilians. After more uncertainty, they told me that if I wished to continue in the program until September, I had to deploy to Afghanistan immediately, but I first had to go to language and culture proficiency classes. I could not believe what I was hearing. First of all I could not just pack and leave, but more importantly they had no idea that I am an Afghan native, speak the languages, and had already served two tours in Afghanistan. God save us from nincompoops in Washington!

In April of 2014, with a heavy heart, I decided to leave the program. I had tried very hard to contribute to the Afghanistan effort, which I still believe to be an important foreign policy and national security issue for the United States. But unfortunately my efforts got lost in the labyrinth of a colossal bureaucracy.

CHAPTER 19

3.4.2015
Afghanistan in Transition

Years of conflict due to external and internal dynamics has profoundly damaged the societal fabric and the psyche of Afghanistan and its people. As a result, the country's societal cohesion, its formal governmental, and its informal traditional institutions were destroyed. The United States launched Operation Infinite Justice, which was later renamed Operation Enduring Freedom, in October 2001. This intervention took place under the banner of a wider effort, the Global War on Terror. Although Al-Qaeda and their protectors, the Taliban, were driven out in a matter of weeks, Operation Enduring Freedom had one major flaw which will make the job of stabilizing Afghanistan very difficult. The United States and its initial partner, the United Kingdom, came in with insufficient forces. They, therefore, relied heavily on and partnered with the warlords of the Northern Alliance and their militias for the assault on Kabul. Other warlord mujahedeen and their militias then became active in the south and the east.

What was left of Afghanistan after the defeat of the Red Army and the fall of the communist regime of Najibullah, the warlords had destroyed by fighting each other for power. Ordinary Afghans fell victim to the pillage and utter lawlessness that resulted from the establishment of fiefdoms by these groups. These events catalyzed the arrival of the Taliban, which the Afghans initially welcomed as needed relief from the warlords. However, the destruction of the country continued unabated. Consequently, the majority of Afghans had nothing but disdain for these maligned actors who we then helped come to power again. The warlords who became well entrenched in the Government of the Islamic Republic of Afghanistan (GIRoA) then had more power than ever to reconstitute and continue the culture of impunity and corruption. This combined with bad governance, lack of rule of law, and the inability of GIRoA to provide basic services to people alienated many Afghans. The Taliban from their safe havens in Pakistan exploited this dissatisfaction to become resurgent by 2005 and 2006.

In effect, the United States and its partners gave the former warlords a de facto legitimacy. These maligned actors also acquired new powers as part of the new Afghan government. They then had a free hand to recreate the culture of impunity and corruption. Disaffected Afghans began to think that the United States and the international community were complicit and were therefore a fair target, akin to GIRoA.

The United States and its coalition partners in the fourteen years since their entry in 2001 have helped the GIRoA and the people of Afghanistan to assume full responsibility for the affairs of their country. The United States and its coalition partners have helped Afghans make inroads toward establishing better and more professional security forces, educating their young, and providing better health care, and so on.

President Obama defined our national goals in Afghanistan as follows:

1. Disrupt, dismantle, and eventually defeat Al-Qaeda and its affiliates and prevent their return to Afghanistan.
2. Strengthen Afghanistan so that it can never again be a safe haven for international terrorism.

Al-Qaeda and its affiliates in Afghanistan have been disrupted and dismantled. Although progress toward strengthening Afghanistan has been made, many serious challenges remain in 2015 which could reverse the gains. The challenges include rampant and endemic corruption, narcotic cultivation and export, lack of basic services and good governance, and the continued culture of impunity. However, the gains came with a heavy cost in terms of blood and treasure, both on our side as well as the Afghan side. Any reversal of the progress made to date will be very detrimental for the United States, the rest of the world, and for the Afghans.

At the end of 2014, Afghanistan assumed full security responsibility. Although the presidential elections were mired with allegations of impropriety, they eventually led to a government of national unity with Ashraf Ghani as the president and his rival Abdullah Abdullah, the chief executive officer. This compromise was brought about by intense pressure on all parties from US Secretary of State John Kerry. A compromise cabinet was finally announced in January 2015, four months after Ghani's inauguration as the new president. Afghanistan's constitution has no provision for a chief executive officer, which makes the longevity of this arrangement an open question. The success of this government in bringing an inclusive political environment, marginalizing or ousting the maligned actors from the government, and curbing the culture of impunity and corruption will boost the confidence of Afghans in their ability to defend themselves and consolidate their gains for building a foundation for their country. This foundation needs to be solid enough to withstand the future challenges Afghanistan will face during the transformational decades (2015 to 2030) to finally reemerge as a secure and viable nation-state devoid of safe havens for international terrorism, at peace with its neighbors, and friendly to us.

The Resolute Support Mission (RSM), with its mandate to train, advise, and assist, will provide the right space for the Afghans, in the context of their expanded responsibilities, to continue consolidating their gains. It can be viewed as an insurance policy against any reversal, provided GIRoA becomes politically more inclusive and is able to make significant progress with regard to anticorruption and other institution building efforts.

Who is fighting who in Afghanistan? From a macroscopic view point there are three overlapping conflicts: the United States and Al-Qaeda, the United States/international community and Afghan Taliban, and GIRoA and Afghan Taliban.

The conflict between the United States and Al-Qaeda is global in scope. While Al-Qaeda and its affiliates are still capable of mounting some headline-grabbing attacks mostly on soft targets such as the Westgate shopping center attack of September 2013 in Nairobi, their capabilities in South Asia have been considerably diminished. The United States is well capable of keeping the pressure on Al-Qaeda by police action and surgical operations to bring the culprits to justice or otherwise keep them in check. Terrorism will not be completely eliminated from the world, and the cooperation of many nations is required to minimize its effect. One proven and effective way to diminish terrorism is to eliminate terrorist breeding grounds, which are usually failed and lawless states. One aim of our continued involvement in Afghanistan through RSM is to ensure Afghanistan continues to be secure and therefore able to deny the terrorists safe havens.

The United States' conflict with the Taliban initially arose due to the Taliban's support and protection of Al-Qaeda. This conflict temporarily came to a stop as the Taliban were driven from power. The United States and its coalition partners became embroiled in direct combat for a second time with a resurgent insurgency whose aim was to topple GIRoA as the nascent Afghan National Security Forces (ANSF) were not sufficiently capable of taking responsibility for the security of the country.

The real combatant parties are GIRoA and the Taliban. The Taliban claim that their conflict with GIRoA and by extension with ISAF is a war of national liberation similar to the Soviet invasion of the 1979. But the facts do not support their claim. A legitimate GIRoA with relatively well trained security institutions can effectively deal with this challenge.

The interference by Afghanistan's neighbors, especially Pakistan, creates the internal grievances that fuel the Taliban insurgency. The Taliban have been very successful in convincing their supporters in much of the Pashtun belt in the east and south of Afghanistan that they (Pashtuns) are under attack by the former Tajik warlords who control GIRoA. They further believe that Karzai sold out to the Northern Alliance Tajiks and that the United States and the international community are complicit in creating this situation.

Pakistan and Afghanistan have shared a historic dispute since the inception of the state of Pakistan in 1947. The dispute is centered on Afghanistan's refusal to recognize the current de facto boundary known as the Durand Line between the two countries. While Pakistan would have fomented and supported weakening the Afghan government in the 1950s,

1960s, and 1970s, it could not do so because there were no internal grievances in Afghanistan to exploit. This was due to the fact that Afghanistan had a legitimate and strong central government acceptable to and supported by the majority of Afghans. Afghanistan was a viable nation-state well capable of defining its territorial integrity.

The former warlords, who include the leaders of the mostly Tajik Northern Alliance as well as some Pashtuns who were driven out by the Taliban in the 1990s, hold all the important positions in GIRoA. The warlords and their corrupt system of patronage continue to perpetuate the culture of impunity. Furthermore, the former warlords have generously benefitted from the largesse of the United States' and the international community's developmental and military aid to Afghanistan over the last fourteen years. The Taliban have successfully used this narrative to recruit foot soldiers and supporters.

When GIRoA attempts to discredit the Taliban through television and other media on religious grounds, it does not resonate with the rank and file disgruntled Afghans. These people believe that GIRoA's deeds speak louder than its declarations and those deeds which consist of corruption and other excesses are contrary to Islamic teachings. As a result, the Afghan government comes across as hypocritical.

Conflicts don't usually come to an abrupt end due to termination and/or resolution. They tend to fade away over time depending on factors such as financial/physical support from patrons; grievances fueling the conflict; unilateral disengagement, such as the United States/Vietnam conflict and the Soviet withdrawal from Afghanistan; or war fatigue; among other things.

The end of conflict in Afghanistan will involve both conflict termination and resolution as a function of the warring sides. Therefore, it is important to identify the parties in the conflict as outlined above.

The United States/international community/Al-Qaeda conflict, which is global in nature, will continue for an undetermined time. The United States/international community/Taliban conflict stems from the coalition's support for GIRoA and as such can be terminated. For the GIRoA/Taliban conflict to conclude, however, both conflict termination and eventual resolution (national political reconciliation) will have to occur. Therefore, it is up to the Afghans to achieve this, and it may not happen in the near future. History has shown time and again that conflicts between indigenous factions of a country or a region can only be resolved by the very factions involved in the conflict.

A strong case can be made that the conditions for the United States/international community/Taliban conflict to terminate have been achieved and RSM will be a powerful catalyst to move the termination forward with a more desirable outcome than an abrupt unilateral disengagement:

- The United States and the international community have partially achieved the objective of building ANSF, which could be instrumental as one important component of GIRoA's effort to meet the challenges of the insurgency post-2014.
- The United States and the international community have helped GIRoA make some progress in the areas of economic development infrastructure, education, health care, and other necessities of the country.
- The United States and its partners were able to deny Afghanistan as a safe haven for Al-Qaeda and drive out the Taliban from power.
- The United States and the international community will continue to provide economic and technical support post-2014.

After the initial intervention to oust the Taliban and Al-Qaeda, the United States became embroiled in the conflict to help GIRoA in its internal conflict until its nascent ANSF was sufficiently capable of taking responsibility for the security of its country.

Our continued involvement under the umbrella of RSM is to provide training, advice, and assistance to the ANSF and other institutions. If the mission is conducted in close cooperation with GIRoA, it will strengthen Afghanistan's national security. The ultimate aim is the ANSF, under a legitimate and inclusive Afghan civilian control, being capable of effectively addressing security challenges anywhere in the country. The capabilities of ANSF will be conditioned on building a solid foundation, sustainable and irreversible.

RSM, with its intent to be a noncombat mission, could empower ANSF and other institutions in Afghanistan to further consolidate the gains of institutional building. This in turn could help GIRoA with building credibility and to be seen as the legitimate representative of the majority of Afghans. GIRoA would then be in a stronger position to influence its internal conflict termination with the Taliban. Conflict termination would bring about security in most of the country, and any minor lingering challenges could be dealt with by a confident ANSF. This would provide the time and space for additional national political reconciliation, resulting in the eventual Afghan conflict resolution.

Why is the continued engagement of the United States and the international community in Afghanistan important? The United States along with the coalition partners including the Afghans have invested heavily, in terms of thousands of lives and vast amounts of money, in Afghanistan and its future. Even if we are prepared to accept no return on the investment, there are other reasons which make a unilateral and sudden departure undesirable. While predicting the future and influencing an ideal outcome may not be possible, without a continued engagement such as RSM the chances of an undesirable outcome would increase. An abrupt disengagement would not only deal a blow to the credibility and commitment of the international community to a more peaceful and orderly world, it could become a catalyst for a new deteriorating security and political situation resulting a new chaotic atmosphere in Afghanistan and elsewhere.

Analysis in the Context of Post-2014 Afghanistan

In the context of post-2014 Afghanistan, RSM can help the country to continue its efforts to improve its deficiencies that still persist in many areas including political stability, security, institution building, elimination of corruption, counternarcotics measures, and development. Eliminating the deficiencies will be a significant contributing factor in strengthening the country's foundation to emerge as a viable nation-state in the transformational decades and beyond.

As I mentioned above, the termination and resolution of the internal Afghan conflict (GIRoA/Taliban) is a moving target and is the responsibility of GIRoA and Afghans to pursue and attain. The United States and its coalition partners have helped GIRoA and the ANSF to deny the insurgency a vote by force until GIRoA can make the necessary political reforms to set the conditions for conflict resolution.

Afghan history has many examples of dealing successfully with internal insurgencies or uprisings without the help of other parties when the governments at the time had legitimacy in the eyes of the constituents. The following cases are examples:

- Amir Abdul Rahman Khan (the Iron Amir) defeated the rebellious Duran and Ghilzai Pashtun tribes and forcibly repatriated many of them to the north and west of the country in the 1880s. He also put down a Hazara insurgency. In 1866 he sent troops to Kafiristan (Nuristan today) and forcibly converted them to Islam.
- In 1945, the Safi Pashtun tribes in Kunar launched an insurgency which the government of King Zahir Shah successfully put down by repatriating the instigators to the north.
- In 1959, the inhabitants of Kandahar City objected to new taxes and the education of girls. The rebellion that ensued was quelled by the government.

In conclusion, as the NATO ISAF mission concludes and GIRoA and ANSF assume full responsibility for the country's security, and in order to ensure the gains achieved over the past fourteen years are not reversed, the international community must remain engaged, albeit under a noncombat posture. RSM, with its mission to train, advise, and assist, can be a useful vehicle to accomplish this. Furthermore, as the sudden disengagement of the United States at the end of the Soviet occupation of Afghanistan helped create the conditions for chaos, which led to a failed state, any sudden and complete disengagement from Afghanistan would:

- Jeopardize the sovereignty of Afghanistan
- Cause the reversal of the gains
- Embolden the extremists in an already volatile region
- Damage the credibility of the United States and its coalition partners

The United States and its international coalition cannot afford another failed Afghanistan which could become a breeding ground for even more extremist groups with much more grave consequences for the world as well as the region.

Sharif Kot ("Sharif's Place")

By
Malaui Mohammad Salim Afi Ana

Colonel Sharif Khan* served his nation
With such courage that it astonished Pakistan

During his time in Gomal he built "Sharif Kot"
With pretty buildings that impress the world

He improved everyone's life including nomadic Kuchi tribes
Along with happy children who had only cried before

What a lucky time for Gomal that Sharif Khan spent time here
May he have a long life and for God to grant him his wishes

What a great temperament Sharif Khan is blessed with
I am not exaggerating my brother, nothing but the truth

His aim is nothing short of doing good for the world
I am touched by him, hence the reason for these words

All the soldiers are happy in Gomal
They are all healthy and live in joy

I can write volumes about Sharif Khan
But I simply congratulate him, we are all so proud of him

Come to Gomal and see for yourself
How so many flowers remain ever colorful, even in autumn

He made Gomal famous
For everywhere you look, you see the flowering legacy of Sharif Khan

* "Khan" is a respectful salutation.

Photo Gallery

My last picture with the late Mayor Hamidi at KPRT.

On the way to Kabul for the second tour.

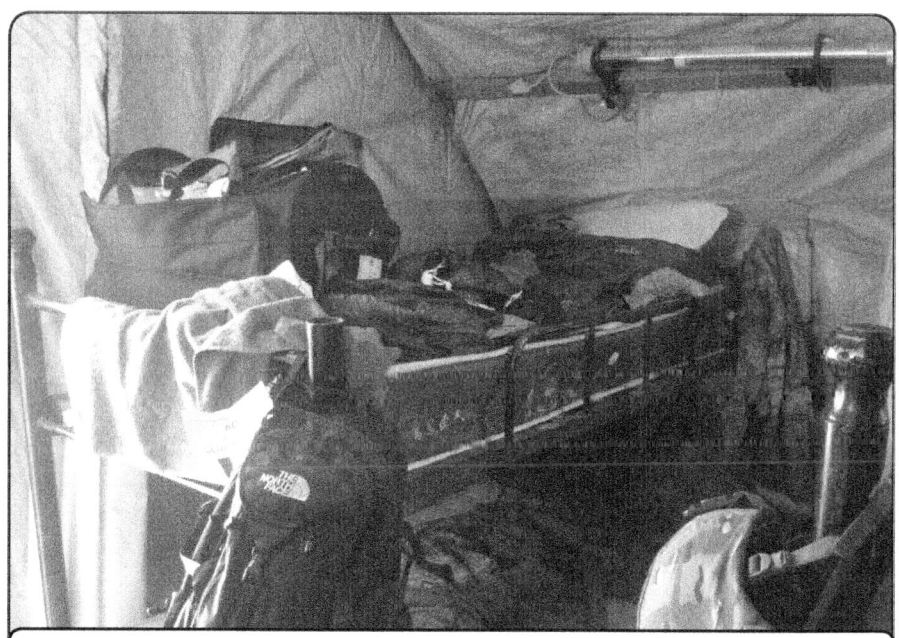

Arrival at Camp Julien to begin my second tour in Afghanistan.

My living quarters on the upper level of the bunk bed with a collapsed mattress.

The once splendid Queen's Palace in Tajbeg, now in ruins.

Tajbeg palace in a 1987 photo from Wikipedia.

With the Kandahar Criminal Investigation Division Director.

Two tired former Talibs, Mujahid and Rohani, on a US helicopter to a peace event in Khost.

With Salangi, the Governor of Parwan. In response to my question about peace, he said: "No, but hell no!"

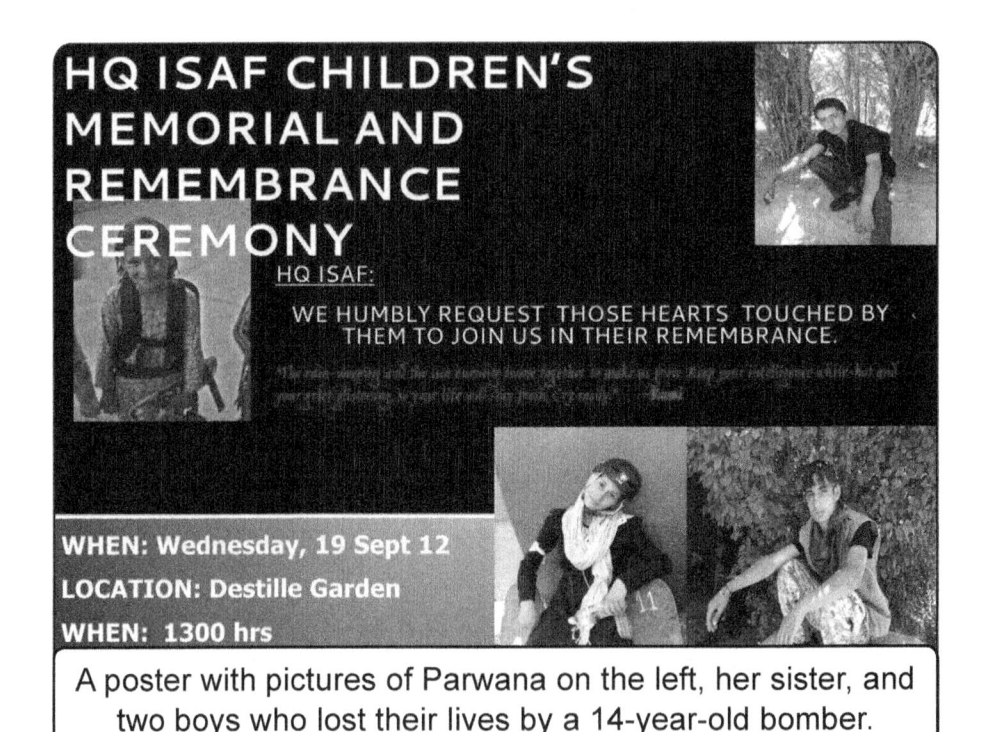

HQ ISAF CHILDREN'S MEMORIAL AND REMEMBRANCE CEREMONY

HQ ISAF:

WE HUMBLY REQUEST THOSE HEARTS TOUCHED BY THEM TO JOIN US IN THEIR REMEMBRANCE.

WHEN: Wednesday, 19 Sept 12
LOCATION: Destille Garden
WHEN: 1300 hrs

A poster with pictures of Parwana on the left, her sister, and two boys who lost their lives by a 14-year-old bomber.

Boys at the peace event in Khost reading a poem about peace with a backdrop of violence.

The late Kandahar Deputy Governor Qadim Patyal talking at a peace event in Nelgham, Zhari. This promising young man was cowardly murdered in 2014 at Kandahar University.

Peace conference in Logar province where women were in attendance also.

From right, the author with three western-educated bright young staff of the HPC, Hashim Alavi, Samai Sadat, and Amin Ramin at the Serena Hotel a day before my departure. Any hope for a better future depends on fine Afghans like these.

With my boss, MG Hook, before his departure.

With former President Karzai after my last meeting at the royal palace (Arg-e- Shahi).

The HPC Chairman, Salahudin Rabbani, at his late father's memorial event. I was his American advisor.

After my last meeting with Chairman Rabbani, saying farewell at his residence.

AUTHOR BIO

My experience includes three decades of international consulting as an aviation engineer in America and Europe, and since 2009 I have worked as a peace diplomat for the US Departments of State and Defense. I'm even more committed now than ever before to peace-building efforts for the international community. What motivates me?

Every individual is born with unique opportunities to better the world. In my case, I was born in Afghanistan during the latter part of its Golden Age, 1930 to the mid-1970s. But who knows of this golden era generated by my family's Mohammadzai clan and Afghans of other backgrounds? Today, not many people, given the barrage of atrocities afflicting war-torn Afghanistan.

I left Afghanistan in November 1976, not to set foot there again until thirty years later as an American citizen. What I saw and experienced when I did return broke my heart—especially having grown up with a happy childhood in Kabul, the capital city.

A keen observer, as both an engineer and a citizen of the world deeply involved in current affairs, I'm impelled to write this memoir from the collection of missives I penned home to family and friends during two deployments in Afghanistan for the State Department (2009–2011) and Department of Defense (2012–2013).

My birth destiny is double-edged. It's a blessing to be able to serve in Afghanistan's reconstruction efforts and build peace bridges between Americans and Afghans. My goal with this book is to convey a sense of what it takes for thousands of Americans performing their daily jobs in Afghanistan amid the myriad challenges and mayhem facing them in a war zone.

I'm also coming full circle to briefly update the history of Afghanistan and of my family, the Mohammadzais. Originally from the southern region of Kandahar, my forebears left for Kabul to help govern Afghanistan a hundred and fifty years ago. My father sacrificed family life to serve as brigade commander to protect the country's eastern border with Pakistan in the early 1960s (while our family remained in Kabul).

Half a century later, I returned as a civilian on behalf of my adopted country—similarly striving to bring peace to Afghans five decades after my father's efforts. It was inevitable, being born a "Sardar." More significantly, the Mohammadzais along with Afghans from all corners of the country were responsible for Afghanistan's Golden Age. Sardar is the aristocratic title of our family clan. Our family tree is included in the Appendix.

APPENDICES

Afghan Cultural Terms

Dari	one of two main languages in Afghanistan, the same as Farsi in Iran but for the accent; a situation that's similar to spoken English in the United States and United Kingdom, but with different accents
Imam	Muslim clergy head
Jihad	fighting others to defend religion, country, and way of life
Jirga	general assembly
Madrassa	Islamic religious school
Mujahedeen	Islamic believers who fight the enemy ("mujaheed" is singular)
Mullah	Muslim priest
Pashtun	the largest Afghan ethnic group stretching geographically from the southwest up to the northeast and parts of the north
Shura	assembly or meeting

Taliban	plural for "seekers" ("talib" is singular)
Ulema	Islamic religious scholars
Ulema Shura	Council of Clergy

Acronyms

AfPak	Afghanistan-Pakistan
AFS	American Foreign Student
ANCOP	Afghan National Civil Order Police
ANP	Afghan National Police
ANSF	Afghan National Security Forces
AOR	area of responsibility
APRP	Afghanistan Peace and Reconciliation Project
BAF	Bagram Air Field
CENTCOM	Central Command
CIVCAS	civilian casualties
CJIATF	Combined Joint Interagency Task Force
CNS	Camp Nathan Smith
COIN	Counterinsurgency
CSAG	Combined Strategic Analysis Group
DFAC	dining facility
DOD	Department of Defense

DV	distinguished visitor
FRI-C	Force Reintegration Cell
GIRoA	Government of the Islamic Republic of Afghanistan
HPC	High Peace Council
HQ	headquarters
IED	improvised explosive device
IJC	ISAF Joint Command
ISAF	International Security Assistance Force
J5	Strategy, Policy, and Plans Directorate
JS	Joint Secretariat, HPC's executive operations arm that provided support for reintegration efforts across Afghanistan
KAF	Kandahar Air Field
KAIA	Kabul International Airport
KPRT	Kandahar Provincial Reconstruction Team
LTC	Lieutenant Colonel
MG	Major General

MRAP	Mine Resistant Ambush Protected armored vehicle that protects soldiers from IEDs
MRE	meals ready to eat (http://mreinfo.com)
NDS	National Directorate for Security
NGO	nongovernmental organization
PRT	Provincial Reconstruction Team
R&R	rest and relaxation
ROLFF-A	Rule of Law Field Force Afghanistan
RSM	Resolute Support Mission
SOF	Afghan Special Operations Forces
USAID	US Agency for International Development
VIP	very important person
VSO	Village Stabilization Operations

Mohammadzai Family Tree

The Barakzai Dynasty
GENEALOGY

Qais ul-Laik ['Abdu'r Rashid Pathan]
(37th in descent from Saul, King of Israel)
Jewish chief of Ghor, converted to Islam by the Prophet Muhammad
I
Ibrahim [Sarabun]
I
Sharf ud-din [Sharakh-bun]
I
Tarīn
I
Malik 'Abdu'l [Abdal]
(ancestor of the Abdalis)
I
Rajjal [Rajor]
I
'Isa

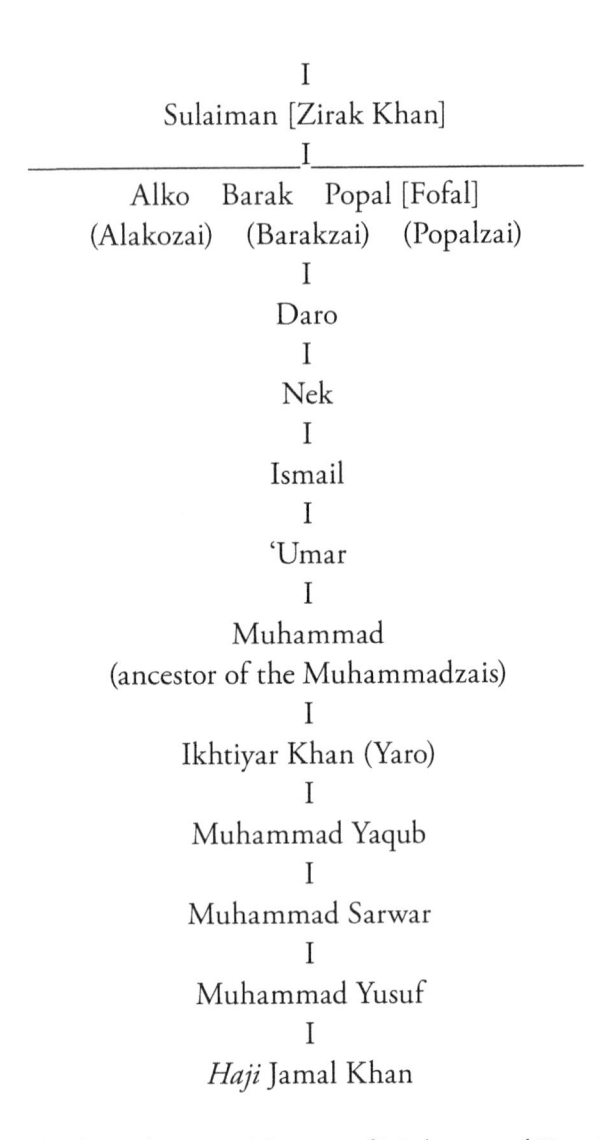

I
Sulaiman [Zirak Khan]
————————I————————
Alko   Barak   Popal [Fofal]
(Alakozai) (Barakzai) (Popalzai)
I
Daro
I
Nek
I
Ismail
I
'Umar
I
Muhammad
(ancestor of the Muhammadzais)
I
Ikhtiyar Khan (Yaro)
I
Muhammad Yaqub
I
Muhammad Sarwar
I
Muhammad Yusuf
I
Haji Jamal Khan

Haji **Jamal Khan**. *b.* 1719, elder son of Muhammad Yusuf. *Topchibashi* (Cdr. of the Artillery forces). *m.* (first) a Barakzai lady. *m.* (second) a Ghilzai lady. He *d.* 1772, having had issue, four sons and a daughter: *Amir ul-Umara*, Sardar **Payinda Khan Muhammadzai**, *Sarfraz Khan. b.* 1758, *educ.* privately. Succeeded his brother as Chief of the Barakzai clan in 1774 and was granted the title of *Sarfraz Khan* by Shah Timur. Appointed *Sardar* of the tribes of Ghilzai, Durrani, etc. Stripped of all his honors and offices 1799. *m.* (first) a lady from the Nusrat-khel branch of the Muhammadzai. *m.* (second) a Malikdinzai Barakzai lady. *m.* (third) a Kohistani lady. *m.* (fourth) a lady of the Nusrat Khel tribe. *m.* (fifth) a lady from the Idu-khel branch of the Hotak Ghilzai tribe. *m.* (sixth) a lady of the Alakozai tribe. *m.* (seventh) *m.* Zainab Begum (*m.* second, 1801, *Sardar* 'Abdu'l Majid Khan), daughter of Musa Khan wakh Jawansher Qizilbash. *m.* (eighth) a Tajik lady. *m.* (ninth) a Siyahposh Kafir lady. *m.* (tenth) a Hazara lady. He was *k.* on the orders of Shah Zaman, for plotting against him, at Kandahar, October 1800, having had issue, twenty-five sons and four daughters:

- 18) H.E. *Sardar* **Said Muhammad Khan**. *b.* 1797 (*s/o* an Alakozai lady). Governor of Khalisajat 1827. *m.* (first) a Barakzai lady. *m.* (second) a Popalzai lady. *m.* (third) a second Barakzai lady. *m.* (fourth) a second Popalzai lady. *m.* (fifth) a third Popalzai lady. *m.* (sixth) a Nurzai lady. *m.* (seventh) a Qizilbash lady. *m.* (eighth) a Yusufzai lady. *m.* (ninth) a second Yusufzai lady. He *d.* 1863, having had issue, twenty-two sons:

h) *Sardar* **Muhammad Husain Khan** (*s/o* the third Popalzai lady). He had issue, one son:

- i) *Sardar* **Muhammad Asif Khan**. *m.* two wives. He had issue, three sons by his first wife, and two sons by his second:
  - (1) H.E. Muhammad Hanif Khan. *b.* 1910 (*s/o* the first wife). Governor of Ghor 1954–1959 and Samangan 1960–1965. *m.* at Kabul, 1938, Saida Bibi, daughter of Said Muhammad Salek. He *d.* 1994, having had issue, five sons and two daughters:
    - (a) Muhammad Aziz Hanif. *b.* at Kunduz, 14 March 1944. Settled in Missouri, USA, before moving to Fairfax, Virginia. *m.* Shaimah Bibi, nee Sharif. He *d.* at Fairfax, Virginia, USA, 2 October 2007, having had issue, two sons and two daughters.
    - (b) Muhammad Rahim Hanif. *b.* at Kabul, 1945.

- (c) Muhammad Karim Hanif. *b.* at Qaleh-ye-now, 1948. Settled in California, USA. *m.* Zarghoona Bibi, nee Assefi. He has issue, two sons.
- (d) Abdul Ghani Hanif. *b.* at Qaleh-ye-now, 1951. Settled in Virginia, USA. *m.* Maryam, daughter of Durmarjan Mesdaq from Paktia. He has issue, two sons and one daughter.
- (e) Fazil Hanif. *b.* at Qaleh-ye-now, 1954. Settled in Virginia, USA. *m.* Moheba Bibi, nee Latifi. He has issue, one son and one daughter.
- (a) Farida Bibi. *b.* at Kabul, 1940. Settled in Brisbane, Queensland, Australia. *m.* Muhammad Zahir Nassiry. She has issue, four children.
- (b) Pashtoona Bibi. *b.* at Qaleh-ye-now, 1957. Settled in Australia. *m.* Rahmatu'llah Asifi. She has issue, three children.
- (2) Lieutenant-General H.E. Muhammad Arif Khan (*s/o* the first wife), *educ.* Mil. Staff Coll., Ankara. Prom. Maj-Gen. 1946, GOC Second Dvsn, Kabul 1946–1948, GOC-in-C Kabul Army Corps 1948, prom. Lieut-Gen. 1949. *m.* Amina Begum, youngest daughter of Brigadier *Sardar* Muhammad 'Ali Khan, by his wife, Humaira Begum [Khore Jan], youngest daughter of Brigadier *Sardar* Fateh Muhammad Khan. He had issue, two sons and one daughter:
- (a) Muhammad Wali Khan Aref. *m.* Suraiya Begum. He had issue, one son and one daughter:
  - (i) Zadran Khan. Christopher Buyers Copyright©
  - (ii) Zahra Khanum.
- (b) Muhammad Tariq Khan Aref. *m.* at Kabul, 17 July 1973, H.H. Princess Humaira Begum [Humaira Wali] (*b.* 1953), eldest daughter of Lieutenant-General H.R.H. *Sardar* 'Abdu'l Wali Khan, GCVO, sometime ADC General to King Muhammad Zahir Shah, by his wife, H.R.H. Princess Bilqis Begum, eldest daughter of H.M.

Al-Mutawakkil Allah, Pairaw ud-din-i-Matin-i-Islam Muhammad Zahir Shah, King of Afghanistan. He had issue, an only daughter:
- (i) Maryam Khanum Wali Aref. *b.* at Rome, 1974. *m.* at Rome, 26 August 1999, 'Umar Khan.
- (a) Fatmah Begum [H.R.H. Princess Fatmah Begum]. *m.* at Kabul, 2 February 1973, H.R.H. Prince Muhammad Daud Pashtunyar Khan (*b.* at Kabul, 14 April 1949), younger son of H.M. *Al-Mutawakkil Allah, Pairaw ud-din-i-Matin-i-Islam* Muhammad Zahir Shah, King of Afghanistan, by his wife, H.M. Queen Humaira Begum, eldest daughter of Colonel H.E. *Sardar* Ahmad Shah Khan, Minister of the Royal Court. She has issue, one son and two daughters - see below.

☐ (3) **Muhammad Sharif Khan** (s/o the first wife Mahboob Begum, she *d.*1951). From first wife Mahboob Begum he has issue, one son and three daughters.
- (a) Mohammad Omar Khan Sharif. *m.* Mary Begum. He *d.* May 1978. He had issue, two daughters:
  - (i) Mariam Omar.
  - (ii) Ogai Omar.
- (b) Hosai Begum. *m.* Khalil Eltizam. Divorced Eltizam. She has issue, five daughters:
  - (i) Helai.
  - (ii) Hasina.
  - (iii) Zohra.
  - (iv) Najia.
  - (v) Marzia.
- Married Ayub Assil. Has issue, one daughter:
  - (vi) Hogai.
- (c) Huma Begum. *m.* Ibrahim. She had issue, one son and one daughter:
  - (i) Ali Khan *d.* 1996 at Brisbane, Australia.
  - (ii) Hawa Begum. Married.
  - (iii) Laima Begum.

- (d) Shaima Begum. *m.* Aziz Hanif. She has issue, two sons and two daughters:
  - (i) Hasib Khan Hanif.
  - (ii) Shaista Begum. *m.* Walid Karim.
  - (iii) Mustafa Khan Hanif.
  - (iv) Mahboob Begum.
- **Muhammad Sharif Khan** (he *d.* August 1976) From second wife Hamida Begum nee Fazel (*b.* 1937) had issue, 2 sons and three daughters:
  - (a) Zarmina Begum Safi. *b.* at Kabul, 1954, *m.* Nour Safi (he *d.* 2013). Divorced. She has issue, two sons:
    - (i) Tareck Safi, *b.* at Kabul, 1973, *m.* Freya Van Onckelen. He has issue, two daughters: Anais *b.* at London 2009; Elisa *b.* at London 2012.
    - (ii) Zmar Safi, *b.* at Bourdeaux 1982.
  - (b) **Abdullah Khan Sharif*** *b.* at Kabul 1955 *m.* Catherine nee Connelly. Has no issue.
  - (c) Belal Khan Sharif. *m.* Mitra nee Miskinyar. Has issue, two daughters:
    - (i) Onai Begum Sharif, *b.* at Virginia, 1990.
    - (ii) Mina Begum Sharif, *b.* at Virginia, 1994.
  - (d) Tooba Begum Sharif. *m.* Curt Mueller. Divorced. Has issue, one son and one daughter:
    - (i) Maximillian Thal Mueller, *b.* at Munich 1994.
    - (ii) Laila Begum Mueller, *b.* at Munich 1997.
  - (e) Zarlasht Begum Sharif. *m.* Eduardo Marx. Has issue, two sons:
    - (i) Constantine (Yaseen) Marx, *b.* at Duesseldorf, 2001.
    - (ii) Sylvester (Rasool) Marx, *b.* at Duesseldorf, 2004.

Source: The Royal Ark (www.royalark.net)

*Abdullah Sharif is the author of this book.